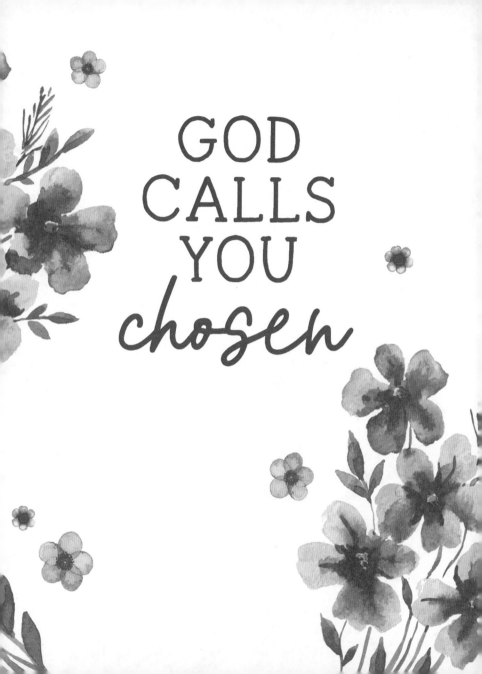

VALORIE QUESENBERRY

GOD
CALLS
YOU
chosen

180
DEVOTIONS
AND PRAYERS
TO INSPIRE
YOUR SOUL

BARBOUR
PUBLISHING

Published by Barbour Publishing, Inc., 1810 Barbour Drive, Uhrichsville, Ohio 44683, www.barbourbooks.com

Our mission is to inspire the world with the life-changing message of the Bible.

Member of the
Evangelical Christian
Publishers Association

Printed in China.

Introduction

Chosen.

Nothing is quite like the feeling of being chosen.

Being chosen is the desire imprinted deep in the heart of every woman. It's the reason we sigh over romantic stories and love to go to weddings. The idea of being chosen as the sole object of a man's affection burns forever in the feminine heart. The tale of Cinderella touches something deep within us because she was chosen at the royal ball over all the other maidens in the land. She was sought after by the prince. This idea of being chosen is really the force behind our pursuit of beauty and charm, behind the dash-after diets and fitness, behind the war against aging and illness. We want to be worthy to be chosen, to be the fairest of them all to someone.

God calls us chosen. Today. Without any changes to ourselves and our setting. We are chosen in Him, loved and cherished. The earthly joys of love between a man and a woman are only a dim reflection of the heavenly template—God is deeply devoted to us, His creation, and He seeks us persistently throughout our lives until we turn to Him and experience His love. He sent His Son, Jesus, to tear down the wall of sin that separated us from Him, and He beckons us to enter a daily relationship with Him.

We can be cherished by God all our lives, whether single or married, young or old. As we open our hearts to His devotion, we are beautified by His grace at work in us. We can see ourselves through His eyes and begin to comprehend His purpose for us.

In these pages, you will find daily inspiration to see the ways in which God has chosen you for Himself. No matter the other messages in your world, you can receive His message of love for you today. See this as a prelude to your daily time in His Word—that is His real message to you.

The Prince is knocking on your door today. He has chosen you and is looking for you. Try on that glass slipper. It will fit you perfectly.

Chosen for Relationship
Made to Know God

God created man in his own image, in the image of God
he created him; male and female he created them.
GENESIS 1:27 ESV

The Creator didn't need us, but He wanted us.

Somehow in the great eternal heart of God there was a desire for relationship with creatures who had both the power to reason and the freedom of choice. So God created man and woman—human beings in His divine image. The Bible hints that God came down to the Garden of Eden and talked with Adam and Eve on a regular, perhaps daily, basis. How amazing that the Creator was actually interested in the thoughts and opinions of the creatures He had made!

The angels are God's servants, His ministers. They were created for service (Psalm 104:4). Humans, however, are created for relationship. There really is no other reason. And when we messed that up, by proxy through the first couple, God wasn't willing to let us go. He found a way to bring us back, to reconcile us to Himself, through the sacrifice of His only begotten Son.

You were chosen to know Him. Like no one else has ever chosen you.

Father God, thank You for choosing to make humankind, for choosing
to make me. I want to reflect Your image well through Your Son,
Jesus Christ. Thank You for wanting to know me. Amen.

Made a Woman

And the rib that the LORD God had taken from the man
he made into a woman and brought her to the man.
GENESIS 2:22 ESV

The Bible tells us that God made a woman on purpose, from Adam's rib, his very body. The significance of that divine surgery is often lost today. Women were made to have relationship, not only with the Creator but with man in the context of marriage. Woman was, in effect, taken from man. She is part of him. Man and woman are halves of a whole: the human reflection of God's image in two complementary modalities—male and female.

While it is true that not every woman today will be part of a marriage relationship, it is important, both biblically and culturally, that we recognize that this context is the basis for how we understand gender. We, men and women, are not the same, but radically, wonderfully different and designed to portray our Creator in opposite yet unifying ways.

Eve was made a woman on purpose for a purpose. God did not intend to make another man to be Adam's companion but a woman. She was chosen to be a woman. So are you.

Creator God, You assign us our earthly form and
gender according to Your plans. Thank You for making
me a woman. I am trusting You to help me discover
that magnificent purpose You have for me. Amen.

Made Finite

*"The secret things belong to the LORD our God, but the
things that are revealed belong to us and to our children
forever, that we may do all the words of this law."*
DEUTERONOMY 29:29 ESV

Eve was created a woman and not a man. She was created human and
not divine. She was created with limitations.

God chose us for limitations. Or maybe He chose limitations for
us. In His wisdom, He created us "this" and not "that."

Humans struggle with our finiteness. It is especially difficult
when our inabilities cut into our plans or when we experience suffering because of them. Perhaps the reason we give ourselves labels
like *atheists* or *feminists* is that we have not yet come to terms with
the limitations of our createdness. We do not agree that God should
have made us this way and not that way. We want it all, no boundaries.
And in a thousand other ways, we balk against our limitations—in our
appearance, in our giftedness, in our blessings.

But this is not our place. It is God's. The secret things belong to
Him, the reasons why. The apostle Paul asked this rhetorical question:
"Will what is molded say to its molder, 'Why have you made me like
this?' " (Romans 9:20 ESV).

The Maker reminds us that our assignment in these bodies is His
to make, and our limitations become beautiful when we accept His
grace to live through them.

*Lord, You have made me for Your glory.
I accept the assignment. In Jesus' name, amen.*

Made for Beauty

"I clothed you also with embroidered cloth
and shod you with fine leather. I wrapped you
in fine linen and covered you with silk."
Ezekiel 16:10 esv

Woman was created to reflect the image of God in beautiful ways as a human female. In the dual, covenantal union with the man, she brings grace and pure loveliness to this portrayal of our Creator. God made her to fill a need in Adam—a need for beauty.

We are designed with a beauty hunger. Our eyes automatically recognize it. Our minds crave it. Our bodies long to be near it.

God likes beauty. He is a God of order and symmetry, of artistic design. The Hebrew word for the creation of Eve is *banah* (Genesis 2:22). It means to build. Woman was not thrown together but carefully and exquisitely crafted by the Master Designer.

And God wants to clothe His daughters with beauty, as in the allegory told by the prophet Ezekiel. He wants to adorn us with His grace and purity, His gentleness and His quiet strength. And He wants us to care for the physical bodies into which He has put us. They contain the valuable soul that is so precious to Him. We were chosen for beauty.

Father, thank You for Your beauty in me. Show me how to
care for it, both on the inside and on the outside. Amen.

Made for Eternity

I know that whatever God does, it endures forever;
nothing can be added to it nor anything taken from it.
ECCLESIASTES 3:14 AMPC

We were chosen for eternal existence, for eternal relationship with the One who made us. It's rather an overwhelming concept, really. God doesn't do disposable—that's an earthly idea.

Some have speculated that God simply could have done away with the first man and woman and started over. But, actually, He couldn't do that. An eternal God created eternal beings in His image. That means they will never cease to be. God could have removed Adam and Eve from this planet, but they would still exist in some form somewhere. Humankind, once conceived, has a never-dying soul and cannot simply evaporate.

So God designed a plan of redemption, a way to honor our eternality and still deal with the sin that separated us from Him. In this way, we are made for eternity twice—first in creation and then in redemption.

Today your world may seem very temporal. Most of our days are filled with everyday stuff—putting dinner in the slow cooker, taking the kids to school or seeing them to the bus stop, driving to work, emptying the dryer or the dishwasher, juggling our budgets and calendars and more. But don't forget, while you manage all your little things, that you are made for big things. You are made for eternal relationship with the God of the universe. He chose that for you.

Lord, I rest today in the knowledge that You are
working out an eternal plan for me. Thank You. Amen.

Made for Purity

Blessed are the pure in heart: for they shall see God.
MATTHEW 5:8 KJV

The Lord our God is the essence of purity. He is absolutely without any trace of pollution. And He wants to replicate this attribute in us.

If you read the laws given in Leviticus and repeated in Deuteronomy, you see that people and clothing and even furniture and utensils were to be cleansed and purified. Bodily cleansing was commanded because God wanted His people to be healthy and beautiful. The cleansing of furniture and utensils and temple items was not only to avoid the spread of disease but also to show that we must cleanse from our hearts and lives any contaminants so that He can dwell with us. The Old Testament tabernacle was a fabric tent; the New Testament tabernacle is us—you and me, temples of the Holy Spirit. The specific application has changed, but the principle remains the same—the Holy Spirit will dwell only in a purified temple. This is just one example of how the Old Testament teaches us unchanging truths about who God is.

You and I are to consecrate ourselves to the Lord so that He may begin His purifying work in us. Only what has been purified by the spiritual application of Jesus' blood in the soul will be ready for the purity of heaven. Those who are pure in heart will see Him.

Almighty God, do Your purifying work in me today. I consecrate myself to You as an earthly tabernacle in Jesus' name. Amen.

Made for Honor

Yet you have made him a little lower than the heavenly beings and crowned him with glory and honor.

PSALM 8:5 ESV

Imagine a warrior returning from battle, having saved the lives of several of his comrades. A ceremony is held, and he receives a medal. The commanding officer pins to the warrior's uniform an ornament that tells everyone he is honored.

God pinned to humankind the ornament of honor. We are made in His image, and that separates us from the animals. One of the most blasphemous aspects of the theory of evolution is that it makes humans out to be only a higher form of animal, devoid of the divine image of the Creator. But God created us a little lower than the angels and higher than the animals.

The present-day focus on animals can be harmful if it causes us to elevate them to a position they are not intended to hold. We are to be thankful for them, to care for them, to use them well, but we are not to worship them or imagine that they deserve the same considerations as humans. They do not have spirits because they were not made in God's image. They are not eternal. We may love them and enjoy them and even grieve when they pass, but we must not value their existence over the lives of the unborn or as equal to the human family.

Men and women were made for a different kind of existence, one crowned with honor.

Father in heaven, please show me how to honor my fellow humans as You do and keep in proper perspective Your beautiful animal kingdom. Amen.

Made for Priesthood

*You yourselves like living stones are being built up as
a spiritual house, to be a holy priesthood, to offer spiritual
sacrifices acceptable to God through Jesus Christ.*
1 PETER 2:5 ESV

As you got dressed this morning, did you think of yourself as a priest? Probably not. But if you belong to Christ, that's who you are.

When God instituted the priesthood in the days of the Old Testament, He gave specific instructions to Moses about who was to serve and how they were to serve. The tribe of Levi was the priestly tribe; serving as priests was their duty and their destiny. And God outlined how they were to dress, how they were to live, how they were to fulfill their ministry. The most important aspect of their responsibility was that they were to speak to God on behalf of the people. The common person could not come into God's presence; he or she would be killed by the awesome holiness that is His essence. But once a year, after going through scrupulous preparation, the high priest would enter the Holy of Holies and make a sacrifice for the sins of the nation.

When Jesus died, the veil of the temple was torn in two from top to bottom, signifying that God would now speak directly to us through Jesus. You and I are made for priesthood, to come into His presence through the power of the blood sacrifice of the cross.

You are chosen for this.

*Jehovah God, thank You for Jesus' making atonement
for me. Today I want to fulfill my priesthood before You. Amen.*

Made for Contentment

If we have food and clothing, with these we will be content.
1 TIMOTHY 6:8 ESV

Magazines and websites that sell fashion and home goods can be black holes into which our contentment vanishes. Our culture thrives on newer and better, on upgrades and makeovers, on more. But this drive speaks to the first lie ever told to a human—God is cheating you; something else will make you happy.

Eve was a perfect woman. She was perfect in every way, and that means she had a perfect mind with which to reason. But she was also susceptible to temptation. And when the serpent introduced the idea that she could have more than God had already given, she bit. Literally. And discontentment invaded our planet like a cancer.

The apostle Paul reminded Timothy, his young son in the faith, that we need to practice contentment with the basics—food and clothing. I think shelter would be considered a fundamental need as well, though Paul was often found in a dungeon and he said that he had learned to be content with little and with much (Philippians 4:11).

The Creator chose us for contentment, to find deep satisfaction in knowing Him and trusting Him to provide the things we need. Jesus referred to this concept when He pointed out that God clothes the grass of the fields and feeds the birds and will also take care of those who trust Him (Matthew 6:26–30).

Today, turn to God for deep peace and joy, for assurance that you are being cared for in remarkable ways.

Lord Jesus, You taught us to depend on the Father for
all our needs. Today I rest in that provision. Amen.

Made for Righteousness

Offer the sacrifices of righteousness,
and put your trust in the LORD.
PSALM 4:5 KJV

We don't use the word *righteousness* too much today, but it packs a punch nonetheless. In the Hebrew, it refers to a sense of rightness, of justice and ethics. A righteous person is one who does what is right in every sense of the word.

Our culture is often satisfied with partial righteousness. In fact, at funerals, and in defense court and other settings, we are accustomed to a person's good points being emphasized and his or her bad points being excused. After all, the reasoning goes, a person can't be perfect in every way.

It is true that no one can be absolutely perfect in the execution of his or her life. But I believe God is more concerned with our deliberate decisions to do what is right in any given situation. We do have choices about that.

You and I were made to be righteous. God didn't craft us to engage in sin or deceit but to live in His light and enjoy the fruits of doing right.

Today we can honor that design by choosing what's right. We can keep our mouths shut when friends are discussing someone in a negative way. We can be pleasant with the very slow store associate. We can give back the extra cash mistakenly handed us by the cashier. We can do what is just and kind and right.

God chose for us to be righteous.

Father, let my words and actions today be deliberate
choices for righteousness. In Jesus' name, amen.

Made for Peace

*"You keep him in perfect peace whose mind
is stayed on you, because he trusts in you."*
Isaiah 26:3 esv

Tension in relationships is stressful. Whether in the home, at work, or in the church, raised emotion and conflict wear us down and erode our stability.

God created us to be at peace. We were not designed to live in stress. In fact, medical science has revealed that there are many detrimental results of being stressed—from headaches and digestive distress to low energy, insomnia, and chest pain.

The frustrating thing, though, is that few of us can actually live stress-free lives. Life seems to come with automatic stressors for each of us. And since this world is broken because of sin, that reality won't change until Jesus changes everything. So the key to enjoying peace is knowing how to handle the stress we have.

The prophet Isaiah gave us insight into this situation—we should focus our minds on God and trust that He can work in the details. Isaiah prophesied that the Messiah would be called the "Prince of Peace." Jesus is the ruler of peace, and He can dispense it. Since we are chosen for relationship with Him, we are chosen for peace. Surrendering our expectations and emotions to Him will help us stay balanced. His Word promises it is true.

*Lord, bring to my heart and mind the peace that only You can give.
I open myself to You. In Jesus' name, amen.*

Made for Fruit Bearing

"You did not choose Me, but I chose you and
appointed you that you should go and bear fruit,
and that your fruit should remain."
JOHN 15:16 NKJV

Saving trees is an activity into which some pour their energies. They are against deforesting and for recycling. They support tree replanting and replacement. They want the trees to have a chance to grow and bear fruit and thus reseed the forests.

God wants us to be strong trees. And He wants us to bear fruit and spread our lives into new sprouts around us. This fruit we are to bear is in the form of godly traits through the Holy Spirit's work in us—the fruit of the Spirit—as well as in the form of little saplings that have sprung to life as new disciples because of our mentoring.

Jesus told His followers and us today that He has chosen us to bear lasting fruit. The way we accomplish this is by staying connected to the source, the Vine, and by allowing His pruning work when needed. As He supplies us with His grace, we can grow stronger and healthier, and at the right time, we will bear fruit and it will remain.

Father, You are the Master Gardener. Cultivate me in all the ways
necessary so I may be fruitful for You. In Jesus' name, amen.

Made for Truth

Lead me in your truth and teach me,
for you are the God of my salvation.
PSALM 25:5 ESV

Truth is like light. When we have it, we can see clearly what we need to do.

The first woman, Eve, was made for truth. It seems she had daily access to the Creator, the source of all truth. Through relationship with Him, she was to be protected from lies. But when she chose to dialogue with the serpent who was more deceitful than any other creature, she took a step toward the darkness and out of the light. As he talked to her, she became more confused and the truth seemed to be obscured. She yielded and accepted the serpent's words. She sinned and then convinced Adam to sin with her. And the planet was plunged into spiritual darkness.

You and I were also made for truth. Because of Jesus and His sacrificial death for us, we can be reconciled to God and walk in truth.

First John 1:7 (ESV) says, "If we walk in the light, as he is in the light, we have fellowship with one another, and the blood of Jesus his Son cleanses us from all sin."

This fellowship with God will help us identify and resist the lies of the serpent. We were made for this. We were chosen for truth.

Father, help me to place myself under the light of
Your Word and Your Spirit. Guide me into ever-
deepening truth. In Jesus' name, amen.

Chosen for Kindness

Put on then, as God's chosen ones, holy and
beloved, compassionate hearts, kindness,
humility, meekness, and patience.
Colossians 3:12 esv

Kindness is more of an action than a feeling.

While compassion is a surge of emotional warmth and sympathy for someone, kindness is the deliberate intervention on behalf of another person. Compassion may prompt kindness, but it is not necessarily part of the equation. In fact, showing kindness to someone for whom we do not have warm feelings is probably the best example of following the Spirit and not our own emotions.

The Bible gives us examples of people who chose to show kindness in their interactions with difficult people. Consider the story of Joseph who spoke kindly to his brothers when he was reunited with them in Egypt (Genesis 50:21). They had hated him and treated him badly, even selling him into slavery. But he chose to speak in kindness to them.

God has also chosen us for kindness. First of all, He has chosen to deal kindly with us, though we have sinned against Him. Second, He has chosen us to show kindness to others, to be extensions on earth of His great love.

Today you will likely encounter someone to whom you can deliberately show kindness. Kindness is often not an automatic response but a chosen one. And if you will make that choice, the God who chose you to reflect Him will give you the strength to carry it out.

Heavenly Father, make me a channel for Your kindness
today. Give me the attitude of Christ, and guide me through
Your Holy Spirit. I ask this in Jesus' name. Amen.

Made for Singing

"The Lord your God is in your midst, a mighty one who
will save; he will rejoice over you with gladness; he will quiet
you by his love; he will exult over you with loud singing."
ZEPHANIAH 3:17 ESV

God designed our vocal cords with the ability not only to speak but also to sing. The vibration of these vocal cords caused by air being forced up from the lungs produces sound waves.

The prophet Zephaniah gave us a glimpse into the feeling God has for His people. Under the inspiration of the Holy Spirit, he described what would happen when Israel was released from captivity and returned to the holy city, Jerusalem. God, her Husband, would be present with her and would rejoice and exult over her with singing. God has such great joy that the Bible describes His response as singing. Likewise, we sing when we're happy.

Through the redemptive work of Jesus, you and I are beloved to God, whether Jew or Gentile. He delights in you. He has chosen you for singing. He has created you to do it. He has given you an example of it. Take every opportunity you have today to sing.

Father God, thank You for loving me and rejoicing over me.
I respond to that by trusting You for salvation and by passing on this
joy to others through my own response of singing. Amen.

Made for Burden Bearing

Bear one another's burdens, and so fulfill the law of Christ.
GALATIANS 6:2 ESV

Have you ever "paid it forward"? You know, have you paid for the drive-through order of the person behind you? In a way, this is a little glimpse into the concept of burden bearing. When you pay it forward, you are taking on the financial responsibility, the burden, of someone to whom you owe nothing. You are willingly assuming the weight of their debt and absorbing the cost of it.

Jesus did that for us when He willingly gave His life for us on a cross. We owed a huge debt to God—the price of our sins. He owed us nothing but took on the cost of our disobedience and paid it for us, satisfying God's justice and giving us peace in the process. Salvation is a free gift to us, but it cost Him dearly.

Admittedly, we will never bear a burden like the one Jesus bore. But in many ways, on a regular basis, we have opportunities to bear the burdens of others, to help support the weight of their bad choices, to lend our strength as they struggle under a debt of irresponsibility.

God chose us to reflect Christ by bearing the burdens of others. Today you may have a chance to "pay it forward" in a new way.

Father, thank You for bearing the weight of my burden through Your Son, Jesus. Open my eyes to opportunities today where I can come alongside someone else. In Jesus' name, amen.

Made for Freedom

For you were called to freedom, brothers. Only do not use
your freedom as an opportunity for the flesh,
but through love serve one another.
GALATIANS 5:13 ESV

We were made to be free to choose—not only to choose our eternal destinies but also to choose our daily actions.

Often when a tragedy occurs because of a sinful choice another person has made (drunk driving, murder, infidelity, child abuse), we are troubled by the thought that God could have stopped him or her from doing that. It would seem to us that it is always right to prevent harm to others. If God can do this, why doesn't He?

What we neglect to see is that to prevent certain events that cause suffering, God would have to violate the free choice He has given someone else. He would have to stop that person from making a free choice in their actions or avert the consequences (which would be, in effect, the same thing). And He will not do that. He has made us in His image with free choice. And it is inviolable.

That's why Paul calls us in this verse to freedom that is bounded by Christian charity. We are not to use our freedom in ways that could hurt others. This is the core of godly liberty and a principle that we must keep in mind.

We were chosen for freedom guarded by love.

Oh God, give me a sensitivity to others so that
I may use my liberty with wisdom and love. Amen.

Made for Assurance

*Let us draw near with a true heart in full assurance of faith,
having our hearts sprinkled from an evil conscience
and our bodies washed with pure water.*
HEBREWS 10:22 NKJV

Women fear abandonment. Perhaps that is because Eve was emotionally abandoned by her husband, Adam, when he blamed her for his sin instead of admitting his own guilt (Genesis 3:12). Perhaps this fear has been passed down to us in our fallen nature.

God promises us assurance of salvation. Because Jesus' perfect sacrifice is sufficient for any sin or failure, we know that we can be forgiven when we ask (Isaiah 1:18; John 6:37; 1 John 1:9). God also promises us assurance of relationship. Because He always keeps His Word, we know that He will never leave us or forsake us (Matthew 28:20; Hebrews 13:5). No matter how black your sky seems today or how shaky the foundation of your life, these two things are settled and sure. Rest in Him.

*Lord Jesus, thank You for keeping Your promises.
I rest in You today for my security. Amen.*

Made for Celebration

As the bridegroom rejoices over the bride,
so shall your God rejoice over you.
ISAIAH 62:5 NKJV

Women love weddings. It's just a fact. There is something about a love story that draws us in. And when you add to it a beautiful gown, a gorgeous venue, and special friends, what's not to love? But the best thing we love about weddings is the cherishing of the groom for the bride. That tender look in his eye, maybe the tears as he watches her walk down the aisle, the gentle way he takes her hand, and even the passion with which he reaches to kiss her—all of these actions speak deeply to our hearts because they tell us she is chosen and cherished. And we love the fact that weddings celebrate this.

We sometimes forget that we are cherished in Jesus' eyes the way a bride is in the gaze of her groom. As a young man chooses a bride, Jesus chooses us. As the groom's eyes are filled with delight in the beauty of his bride, Jesus' eyes are filled with delight when we walk toward Him. As a man cherishes the woman who is about to take his name, Jesus cherishes us as we take His.

You and I were chosen for this celebration of love. Someday there will be a great wedding in heaven when Jesus, the Bridegroom, marries His bride, the Church, and we will understand, finally, how lavish is the love Jesus Christ has for us!

Father, thank You for creating me for cherishing, for a celebration
of love. I look forward to eternity with You. Amen.

Chosen for Blamelessness

He chose us in Him before the foundation of the world,
that we should be holy and without blame before Him in love.

<small>EPHESIANS 1:4 NKJV</small>

Coming home one afternoon, I received a traffic warning from a police officer. Eating my ice cream while driving, I had drifted left of center, and he was concerned. Not wanting a perhaps intoxicated driver on the roads, he pulled me over and nicely, and a bit humorously, issued me a warning. I was not blameless. But at least my offense was unintentional, and he didn't make me pay a fine.

The word *blameless* means "innocent of wrongdoing." It is a wonderful, vindicating word. But it is a character trait we can achieve only through the power of Jesus. In ourselves and with our strength, we will never be able to avoid sin and maintain a surrendered heart. But with His power, we can have pure motives and not choose willful disobedience.

God chose us to be blameless before Him in love. He wants us to know His power at work in our hearts and lives so that we may live in unbroken fellowship with Him.

Long before you or I were born, before the very foundation of the world we live in, God was at work, planning our redemption and relationship with Him. He chose us, and now we can choose Him.

Lord, I can't be blameless in my own power. Give me the
grace and power of the Holy Spirit to avoid evil
and choose You. In Jesus' name, amen.

Chosen for Rejoicing

I rejoice at Your word as one who finds great treasure.
PSALM 119:162 NKJV

Rejoice is a word that makes me think of classical music like Handel's *Messiah*. The aria "Rejoice Greatly," taken directly from scripture in Isaiah, reminds us at Christmastime and any other time that the "King has come to us" and we can rejoice.

We don't use the word *rejoice* much anymore. But when we do, it signifies a significant level of happiness. It even seems to trump its cousin word *joy*. To rejoice is to take intense pleasure in something.

We were made for rejoicing. And one of the things we are to rejoice over is the Word of God. Scripture defines it as living and powerful like a sword, reflecting truth like a good mirror, and pleasant to the taste like honey. It is compared to treasure—valuable, worthy, to be cherished and protected.

God speaks to us through His Word. He will use it to strengthen us, correct us, teach us, and comfort us. He loves us through His Word as we gain deeper understanding of His nature and how He cares about us.

God chose to give us His Word in tactile form, first through the prophets and then through Jesus. And the Bibles we have today are the preserved, sacred Word, chosen to bring us light and life. That is worth rejoicing over.

Father, thank You for giving me Your Word.
I rejoice over its power and truth and beauty today. Amen.

Chosen for Salvation

I have trusted in Your mercy;
my heart shall rejoice in Your salvation.
Psalm 13:5 nkjv

Did you know that the Hebrew word for salvation here means "deliverance"?

That's right. It denotes a rescue, a victory.

Those of us raised around church are accustomed to the language of "being saved from sin." We know that it refers to receiving Christ into our hearts by faith as the atonement for our wrongdoing and for the promise of eternal life. But perhaps we forget that salvation is literally deliverance from the power of Satan, from the dominion of darkness. We might think that refers to those who are involved in witchcraft or debauched sexual sins, but actually, every one of us is a prisoner of Satan until we come to Christ.

We are born sinners, born with a depraved nature that is turned toward evil. God knew that we couldn't rescue ourselves, so He sent a champion, a warrior, a sacrificial lamb. By giving up His life on the cross and then wresting the keys of death and hell from Satan, Jesus conquered the depths of the dungeon for us. Then He rose on the third day so that there would be no doubt that He is the victor.

Now Jesus unlocks the doors of our prison cells when we ask Him. Those cells are labeled many ways—pride, gossip, addiction, unforgiveness, lying, sensuality, anger, bitterness, and more. But He can deliver us from any of them. There is no prison cell to which He does not hold the key.

We are chosen for deliverance in Christ.

Lord Jesus, I am so thankful for the deliverance You bring because of Calvary. I ask You to reveal to me any bondage that currently holds me captive, and please set me free. In Your name, amen.

Chosen for Reconciliation

For if while we were enemies we were reconciled to God by the death of his Son, much more, now that we are reconciled, shall we be saved by his life.

ROMANS 5:10 ESV

Reconciliation is a beautiful word. It sounds like coming home, being wrapped in love as warm as a quilt, sitting down in your usual spot at the family table, and knowing all is well. Reconciliation is redeeming love in action.

Though most of us don't like to think of ourselves in this way, the Bible tells us that we were enemies of God. We were rebels wanting our own way and not His way. We wanted to follow the instincts of our fleshly appetites—instincts for deceit and revenge and pride.

Jesus is the bridge to the Father. He came to Earth and took on human flesh so that He could die for us like we were supposed to die. He took the punishment for our sins. Because Jesus was an absolutely perfect sacrifice, God canceled the charges against us and welcomed us into His family.

Now that we have been reconciled to God, He has chosen us to be ministers of reconciliation. We are to be busy in our world, telling the good news that anyone can accept this free gift and this new family. We were chosen to be both receivers and givers.

Father in heaven, thank You for Your Son, the One who reconciles us through His shed blood. Let me be a channel of reconciliation to others today. Amen.

Chosen for Holiness

Put on the new self, created after the likeness
of God in true righteousness and holiness.
Ephesians 4:24 esv

After my daughter's wedding, I had to launder some of the white tablecloths we'd used at the reception. Wanting to make sure I sent them back to my friend as snowy white as possible, I bought a product I'd never used before. It was a special whitening agent designed to "remove dingies that bleach and oxy can't!"

That's what God wants to work in us—His holiness that removes the impurities we can't and whitens and brightens our souls until His reflection shines clear. A preacher once said that "everything God touches He turns to holy."

God instructed Moses to have the phrase "Holy to the Lord" engraved on the signets worn by the high priest (Exodus 28:36 esv), and Zechariah prophesied a day when the bells on the horses would be inscribed with "Holy to the Lord" and even the pots used would be consecrated to Him (Zechariah 14:20–21 esv).

God wants to give us His holiness through the atoning and purifying work of Jesus' blood applied to us in the Spirit. He wants to remove the spots and stains of self and fill us instead with His love for others. As we surrender our lives to Him, He can begin His holy work in us. We were chosen for holiness.

Lord I want to be holy, pure, and clean inside. I surrender
myself to You; take my stains and replace them
with Your holiness. In Jesus' name, amen.

Chosen for Togetherness

By grace you have been saved—and raised us up with him and seated us with him in the heavenly places in Christ Jesus.
EPHESIANS 2:5–6 ESV

We all need alone time, but most of the time we enjoy activities with friends. Having a girlfriend to shop with and eat with and laugh with makes a fun day even better. God designed us for togetherness. We were intended to be social.

It will be the same in heaven. We will be gathered together with those who have loved Christ throughout all the ages. And we will enjoy social interaction and conversation and even feasting for eternity.

God planned for us to be in close relationship with Him, both here and for eternity.

Heavenly Father, thank You for all You've done to bring me into togetherness with You. I love You. Amen.

Chosen for Womanhood

God Calls You Fulfilled

*By faith Sarah herself received power to conceive,
even when she was past the age, since she
considered him faithful who had promised.*
HEBREWS 11:11 ESV

Infertility is painful in any generation and civilization, but it was especially so in the day when Sarah lived. Children provided status and security for a woman in biblical times. A woman who could not bear a child was often considered to be cursed, and she had no one to care for her in her old age. She was a disappointment to her husband and even a drain on his resources and goodwill. She was not fulfilled.

But scripture says that Sarah considered God to be faithful. We're not sure exactly what that means since we know from Genesis that she laughed when the angel told Abraham that she would have a son (Genesis 18:12). Perhaps it means that she believed Jehovah was able to do what was right for her, that He would bring fulfillment to her life in some way.

None of us wants to be chosen for a difficult path, but sometimes it is the way to fulfillment. We must never forget that He who promised is faithful.

*Lord, You are Jehovah Jireh, my provider. Today, help me
trust that You are working out what I need to be
fulfilled in Your purpose for me. Amen.*

God Calls You Adopted

And the women said unto Naomi, Blessed be the Lord, which hath not left thee this day without a kinsman, that his name may be famous in Israel. And he shall be unto thee a restorer of thy life, and a nourisher of thine old age: for thy daughter in law, which loveth thee, which is better to thee than seven sons, hath born him.

RUTH 4:14–15 KJV

We don't know much about Ruth's childhood or adolescence, but we do know that she was a native of Moab and that she married an immigrant, a Hebrew. Mahlon had escaped the famine in Israel with his father and mother and brother. Israelites were not encouraged to marry pagans who worshipped other gods. Whether Mahlon and his family had been able to persuade Ruth to worship their God, we do not know. But her words to Naomi, "Your God [shall be] my God" (Ruth 1:16 ESV), convince us that she was at least not hostile to learning about Jehovah.

The story of Ruth and Naomi traveling to Bethlehem and her subsequent marriage to Boaz, a wealthy landowner and respected businessman, seems like the stuff of fairy tales. But most astounding of all is that she married into the Davidic line, the earthly lineage through which Jesus, the Messiah, was born.

Ruth was adopted into the family of God. And so are we when we are willing to forsake the other trails of our lives and pursue Jehovah.

Lord God, You are the Father who adopts all who come to You in Jesus' name. Thank You for receiving me. Amen.

God Calls You Seen

*So she called the name of the L*ORD *who spoke to her,*
"You are a God of seeing," for she said, "Truly here
I have seen him who looks after me."
GENESIS 16:13 ESV

God sees lonely women in forgotten places.

Hagar was in the wilderness, pregnant and alone. She had no resources and no way to take care of herself. She was a desolate woman.

But God had His eye on her the whole time. He knew the circumstances of her life. He knew that she had no choice in the larger decisions that had brought her to the present—she was a slave and did not have the freedom to decide her own course. He knew that she had finally gotten one advantage in her life—she was pregnant with the child of the great man Abraham. He knew that she had let it go to her head. After being managed and manipulated and controlled her whole life, she now had a chance to get things her way. The luxuries of Sarah's life could not give her what Hagar now enjoyed—status as the mother of Abraham's child. Who could blame her for squeezing every bit of pleasure and pampering from that?

But God still had a plan, and He sent an angel to tell her to return to Abraham's caravan. He promised recognition for the son she carried. It would be a notorious recognition, but he would not be overlooked as she had been.

Wherever you are today, God sees you. He is aware of your background and advantages and disadvantages, your story and your future. He has His eye on you.

Lord God, my life is open to Your eyes. You are El Roi:
The God Who Sees Me. Show me what to do. Amen.

God Calls You
a Participator

And she said, "According to your words, so be it."
Then she sent them away, and they departed.
And she tied the scarlet cord in the window.

Joshua 2:21 esv

Rahab wasn't part of the original story, but she became an important addition to it. She was raised in a pagan environment and involved in a salacious occupation. She was not the usual type for the cast of God's story. But faith in God changes the script of our lives.

When the two spies showed up at her door, Rahab had already been thinking about Israel and the astounding news that had reached Canaan about them. Somehow, in her heart, she had decided that these people must have the power of God with them, a power greater than those of the heathen deities to which her people prayed. Perhaps that is why she didn't turn them in to begin with. Instead, she gave them refuge and then hid them when the officials came conducting a search. When all was clear, she appealed to the spies for her own life and the lives of her family. And they made a deal. Rahab married an Israelite and gave birth to a son they named Boaz, who also married a redeemed foreigner. This ancestry was the earthly line of Jesus, the Messiah.

Don't think that your past precludes you from participating in God's story. Faith in Christ will redeem your narrative and include you in the greatest plot ever! You are chosen to be a participator!

God, thank You for the power of redemption. I want to
participate in Your great plan today! In Jesus' name, amen.

God Calls You
to Adventure

"For if you keep silent at this time, relief and deliverance will rise
for the Jews from another place, but you and your father's
house will perish. And who knows whether you have not
come to the kingdom for such a time as this?"

ESTHER 4:14 ESV

Little did Esther know that her adult life would be one of the most incredible stories in the Bible. Her parents died when she was young, and that is why she was living with her uncle Mordecai. As an adolescent, she developed remarkable beauty; perhaps she was the girl whom all the neighborhood boys flocked around, the one whom all of them wanted to win. But all the normal trajectory of life changed when Queen Vashti was dethroned and the king's men were sent out to gather young women as prospects for the king.

The story of how Esther won over the hearts of those around her and succeeded in captivating the king as well is a testament not only to modest and winsome femininity but also, and mainly, to God's plan for her. And her adventure continued as she saved the king's life and then saved her peoples' lives through her willingness to risk her own life to speak on their behalf.

Esther's adventure was planned by the same God who calls you today to follow the steps He is laying out for you. It will be different from hers but remarkable in its own way. He has chosen you for it.

Father, today I say yes to Your plans and purposes for me.
I say yes to Your adventure through Your Son, Jesus. Amen.

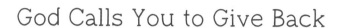

God Calls You to Give Back

"For this child I prayed, and the Lᴏʀᴅ has granted me my petition
that I made to him. Therefore I have lent him to the Lᴏʀᴅ.
As long as he lives, he is lent to the Lᴏʀᴅ."
1 Sᴀᴍᴜᴇʟ 1:27–28 ᴇsᴠ

Many women in the Bible struggled with infertility. And it was always seen as a supernatural act when a woman who was barren was then able to conceive. Genesis 30:22 says, "God. . .opened her womb" in reference to Rachel. In Genesis 21:1 (ᴇsᴠ) we read that "the Lᴏʀᴅ visited Sarah. . .and. . .did to Sarah as he had promised." And in 1 Samuel 2:21 (ᴇsᴠ), "the Lᴏʀᴅ visited Hannah, and she conceived." Conception of new life is not on our terms but on God's.

Hannah vowed to the Lord that if she would conceive, she would literally give her son back to Him in service in the temple. And she did. According to the times when children were weaned in those days, Samuel was probably around five years of age when his mother took him to live with the old priest Eli. She was giving back what God had given her.

What blessing do you hold today that God wants you to offer back to Him? It may be a relationship or a material item or your status or position.

God calls us not only to the exciting things but also to the sacrificial things. Lift up to Him your offering today.

God, You have blessed me with this, and today I hold it
up to You. Do with it what You will. I trust You. Amen.

God Calls You a Mediator

*And David said to Abigail, "Blessed be the LORD,
the God of Israel, who sent you this day to meet me!
Blessed be your discretion, and blessed be you,
who have kept me this day from bloodguilt and
from working salvation with my own hand!"*
1 SAMUEL 25:32–33 ESV

Because God is the author of reconciliation, He calls us also to be involved in bringing reconciliation (2 Corinthians 5:18). This is very near to His heart. Estrangement between a husband or wife or family members or church members or friends grieves Him. He calls us to forgive and reconcile (Matthew 5:24; 1 Corinthians 7:11; 12:25). God did not let us stay apart from Him but found a way to reconcile us to Himself through Jesus.

The Bible describes Abigail as beautiful and discerning. But her husband, Nabal, was badly behaved (1 Samuel 25:3). He mishandled a meeting with David's men who had come to ask for provisions in return for their protection of his land in the preceding year. Nabal was belligerent, disrespectful, and flippant, and he flatly denied recognizing the service David had provided. When the men gave their report, David and his men strapped on their swords and prepared to annihilate all the men of Nabal's household.

But Abigail heard about the problem and found a solution. She gathered supplies and met David on the road and averted a tragedy. God used her to mediate an explosive situation.

What situation today can you mediate? With whom can you reconcile? God calls you to it.

*Lord, You are the source of all mediation and reconciliation.
Use me today as a channel through which Your
grace can flow to others. Amen.*

God Calls You to Trust

*So she went away and did according to the word of Elijah;
and she and he and her household ate for many days. The bin of
flour was not used up, nor did the jar of oil run dry, according
to the word of the LORD which He spoke by Elijah.*
1 KINGS 17:15–16 NKJV

She is known in scripture only as the widow of Zarephath. But her story has encouraged many to trust in the God who provides for us when we do His will.

There was a scarcity of food in the land of Israel because God had brought judgment by the word of the prophet Elijah. There had been no rain or dew for a long time, and the gardens and fields were shriveled and barren.

The Lord provided for the prophet by miraculous means, including his lodging with a widow and her son for a certain period of time. But to provide for the prophet, the widow had to use the last bit of ingredients she had, what she had been saving for a last meal for herself and her boy. When she trusted the word of God's man and made him a cake first, her needs were provided for days to come.

One of the names used for God in the Old Testament is Jehovah Jireh: God Provides. This widow, desperate and needy, discovered that Jehovah can be trusted. In what ways do you need to trust Him for yourself today?

Lord, You are Jehovah Jireh. Give me the grace to trust You with the desperate situations in my life today. In Jesus' name, amen.

God Calls You
to Be an Example

*"Assuredly, I say to you, wherever this gospel is preached
in the whole world, what this woman has done
will also be told as a memorial to her."*
MATTHEW 26:13 NKJV

I have often wondered what the woman in Matthew 26:13 thought when she heard Jesus say these words. She had approached the Teacher with her box of fragrant oil and broken its contents on Him. And now her simple act of lavish love was going to be told throughout the whole world. Wow. She wasn't expecting special honor. She was merely expressing her devotion to her Lord. And in doing so, she became a model of surrender.

In our daily expression of commitment to our Lord, we can also be examples. The apostle Paul said to the churches he served, "Imitate me, just as I also imitate Christ" (1 Corinthians 11:1 NKJV). We are to live our lives in such exemplary and devoted ways that other believers can imitate our lives and acts of service and thereby bring glory to God.

Maybe there is something God is putting on your heart today that He can use as an example to others. Don't do it to be seen by others; do it out of love for Him. Then let Him decide to use it however He wants.

*Lord Jesus, I want my life to bring honor to You as I express
my love in acts of service to others. Use me for Your
own glory in any way You choose. Amen.*

God Calls You Rescued

*When Jesus rose early on that first day of the
week, he appeared first of all to Mary of Magdala,
from whom he had driven out seven evil spirits.*
Mark 16:9 Phillips

Few of us have experienced or witnessed observable demon possession, but most of us have read about it in the Bible. Those who have served in missions in other countries have sometimes encountered overt demonic activity, but often, in more advanced countries, this kind of spiritual oppression is evidenced by perversion and addictions in the population. However, when Jesus walked the earth, demonic activity was common. And the evil spirits avoided any kind of interaction with Him, sometimes begging Him not to send them away into hell.

The Bible doesn't tell us how Mary Magdalene (as she is known) came to be demon possessed or how it was evidenced in her life, but it does tell us that Jesus delivered her from them. She became a devoted follower, transformed by the rescuing power of the Messiah.

Something may be holding you captive today—depression, grief, an addiction to pornography or some other indulgence, the guilt of an abortion, the trauma of abuse, marital conflict, or parenting challenges. Satan often works through these pathways to keep us from freedom.

Turn to Jesus. He calls to rescue you through the power of the cross.

*Oh God, I come to You today with my oppression. I call it by name:
[name oppression]. Please deliver me in the name of Jesus. Amen.*

God Calls You
to Show Mercy

Jesus answered and said to her, "Whoever drinks of this water will thirst again, but whoever drinks of the water that I shall give him will never thirst. But the water that I shall give him will become in him a fountain of water springing up into everlasting life."

JOHN 4:13–14 NKJV

Ethnic divisions were a problem when Jesus was on earth, as they have been since the Tower of Babel when God separated humans into people groups. Because the people of Samaria were a mixed race, they were hated by both Jews and Gentiles alike. The Jews considered them a mongrel breed and avoided even walking through the area of Samaria when traveling, which is why the Bible says that Jesus "needed to go through" Samaria (John 4:4 NKJV).

The woman who came to the well that day as He rested there was aware of the racial tension between them. She must have been surprised that He didn't leave as soon as she approached. And she was probably even more shocked when He spoke to her, breaking the gender code of the time. But because He did, she found mercy. She found a new life in Christ.

You and I are called to break lines of separation and reach out to those who need mercy. If God gives us the opportunity to share this "living water" with those whose lives are parched and empty, we must do it, no matter the other barriers we may face. We are called to show mercy.

*Lord, give me compassion for all those who don't know You.
Use me to show mercy in Your name. Amen.*

God Calls You to Joy

*Then [Jesus] came and touched the open coffin, and those who
carried [the boy] stood still. And He said, "Young man, I say to
you, arise." So he who was dead sat up and began to
speak. And He presented him to his mother.*

LUKE 7:13–15 NKJV

The loss of a child is a woman's ultimate sorrow.

When she has carried that life in her body for nine months and in
her heart for a lifetime, she does not part with it easily. When death
rips it from her grasp, the hole remains.

Luke the physician writes in his Gospel account about a funeral
procession that Jesus interrupted. The mother was a widow and the
young man on the bier was her only son. She was now totally alone,
without someone to provide for her. She was lonely. She was grieving.

Jesus saw this devastated mother and changed the course of life
for her. With life-giving words, He raised the son to life and called the
mother from sorrow to joy.

There are times when God does not give back our loved ones or
avert a tragedy or save our jobs or homes from disaster. In those times,
He calls us to a different kind of joy—a deep security in knowing Him.

But either way, we are called to delight ourselves in His power and
to expect the unexpected. When He speaks, what is dead in us must
live again.

*Lord Jesus, You raised the dead through Your life-giving power.
Today I bring You my griefs and sorrows. Give me the security
to know You will do what is best. In Jesus' name, amen.*

God Calls You to Leadership

And on the Sabbath day we went out of the city to the riverside,
where prayer was customarily made; and we sat down and spoke
to the women who met there. Now a certain woman named
Lydia heard us. She was a seller of purple from the
city of Thyatira, who worshiped God.
ACTS 16:13–14 NKJV

Purple was more than a color in ancient times; it was an item, a luxurious item. Purple fabric, often purple silk, was difficult to obtain and thus an expensive commodity. Lydia was a businesswoman, a merchant. But she was also part of a group of women who met by the river to worship. And when she heard the good news about Jesus, the Bible account tells us that her heart was opened and she and her household were baptized. She hosted Paul and his traveling companions in her home when they ministered in Philippi.

Lydia was a woman with leadership skills and business acumen. The Lord used her in establishing a church in Philippi that soon came to include a slave girl who was freed from demonic possession and a jailer who was saved after an earthquake. These and many others were part of a family of new believers in the city.

Perhaps leadership opportunities are confronting you. If you can help your church leaders in strengthening your local church, do it. God may be calling you to it.

Father God, You give opportunities to each of us that fulfill
Your will in the Church. Help me to be obedient to
walk through the doors You open. Amen.

God Calls You to Mothering

*The man called his wife's name Eve [life spring],
because she was the mother of all the living.*
GENESIS 3:20 AMPC

As a woman, you are called to mothering. . . . Yes, even if you are not a biological mother.

You have been gifted with a feminine identity and maternal traits; you are to use them in ways that reflect the nurturing, gentle heart of our God. A draw to nurturing is an almost universal trait in women. A few may struggle with it, and sometimes that is due to childhood trauma or improper imprinting with a feminine role model. But for most of us, nurturing is natural—we dote on everyone who needs care, from puppies to babies.

Adam recognized this important aspect of his wife's nature and named her to reflect it. She was Eve—a spring of life. This is especially true because everyone who has ever lived since has descended from her. But it is true of each of us that we can reflect the life-giving, nurturing attributes of the divine image in which we were created.

When you choose kind words in a conflict with someone at work, you are giving life. When you forgive and forget a little insult, you are giving life. When you give encouraging words to the sales associate, you are giving life. When you buy a cup of coffee for a friend or take groceries to a homeless shelter, you are giving life. When you pray for the people in your life because you care about their needs, physical, emotional, or spiritual, you are giving life. Look for ways to use your mothering skills today. You are called to it.

*Heavenly Father, I am created in Your image, to reflect the aspects
of Your divine nature that You chose for the earthly female.
Help me today to be faithful in fulfilling that call. Amen.*

God Calls You to Honor Singleness

I wish that all men were like I myself am [in this matter of self-control]. But each has his own special gift from God, one of this kind and one of another. But to the unmarried people and to the widows, I declare that it is well (good, advantageous, expedient, and wholesome) for them to remain [single] even as I do.

1 Corinthians 7:7–8 ampc

But He said to them, Not all men can accept this saying, but it is for those to whom [the capacity to receive] it has been given. For there are eunuchs who have been born incapable of marriage; and there are eunuchs who have been made so by men; and there are eunuchs who have made themselves incapable of marriage for the sake of the kingdom of heaven. Let him who is able to accept this accept it.

Matthew 19:11–12 ampc

Let's begin by affirming marriage. God created it as the foundation of society, and it is honorable in all (Hebrews 13:4). But Jesus Himself, as well as the apostle Paul, affirmed the dignity and worth of singleness, and so should we.

Many single people do not see singleness as the special gift that Paul calls it, but it is certainly true that when it is played well, the role of single adult shines brightly for Christ. Let us honor this life—in us or in others.

Father in heaven, show me how to honor singleness as a gift and as a way of life elevated because Jesus lived it. In His name, amen.

God Calls You to Be an Orphan

We have become orphans and fatherless.

LAMENTATIONS 5:3 AMPC

Being fatherless has never been seen as a good thing. In fact, down through time, it was a reason to be shunned in polite society. If one did not even merit having the last name of a responsible man, he or she was considered an outcast. Orphans were treated in much the same way, often suspected of having less moral fiber than other children and shuffled around in careless fashion.

Because of their delicate situation in society, God gave special instructions to Israel about the care of the widows and the fatherless. And the New Testament also commends ministry to them (Exodus 22:22; Deuteronomy 24:21; Psalm 82:3; James 1:27).

The scripture in Lamentations is concerning the captivity of Israel. They saw themselves as spiritually bereft because of their difficulties. And, of course, not all of us are actual orphans. But when we see ourselves in that kind of need, we can come to our heavenly Father with expectant faith.

Our dependence on Him is to be much like that of an orphan who looks up into the face of her adoptive father. She knows she is finally chosen and loved and that he will give her what she needs to be safe and whole. He will not mistreat her because of her unfortunate situation.

God calls us to this degree of expectation from Him. We are spiritual orphans; He is our adoptive Father.

Father, I lift my face to You and acknowledge my need of You in my life. Thank You for choosing me. Amen.

God Calls You to Old Age

Even to your old age, I am He,
and even to gray hairs I will carry you!
Isaiah 46:4 NKJV

Aging is not a season of life about which we are excited. In fact, most of us try to delay it as long as possible and counteract its effect on our minds and bodies. There is no shame in that. We were not made for aging; we were made for eternal existence. The soul resists the decay of earthly aging. We wish to transcend the dust of time. But since our world is fallen, aging is one of the consequences, and God calls us to it in due season.

Western culture admires and glorifies youth. The loss of youth is seen as a terrible tragedy and in some ways akin to a loss of worth. But God says that in our aging, He is the same. He is our Companion and Helper, our Refuge and Strength, just as He was when we were young. And He will "carry" us through the gray hair and wrinkles, the pudgy belly and ankles, the watery eyes, the papery skin, the dementia, and the pain. He will be there, faithful in the season that introduces us to the life thereafter.

Babies emerge from the womb wrinkled and sometimes a bit ugly. Humans emerge from death into heaven the same way. But one breath of heaven's air transforms the ugliness into unending beauty. This is the life to which God calls us.

God, You are ageless; I am not. But You have promised
Your presence with me in every season. I can look
ahead, secure in that knowledge. Amen.

God Calls You an Immigrant

Beloved, I urge you as sojourners and exiles to abstain from the
passions of the flesh, which wage war against your soul.
1 Peter 2:11 esv

One of the most fascinating places in America is Ellis Island in New York Harbor. The immigration center there has a fascinating history, having processed approximately twelve million arrivals from 1892 to 1924. Every one of those people entered those gates with trepidation, with hopes and dreams. Some of them were, sadly, unable to enter the land of promise. But many more were. It is more than likely that most of us have an ancestor or two who arrived during that period of time.

Immigration is a complex journey and process. It has always been associated with challenges and unforeseen complications. And God's Word instructs us to be kind to those who are strangers among us.

As a child of God, you are an immigrant in this world. You are on your way to the real land of promise. And if you know Jesus, you are assured of entry. You will have no complications with your paperwork that is stamped with His name.

The apostle Peter reminds us that because we are not truly citizens of this world, we are to conduct ourselves in godly ways, ways that reflect our heavenly status.

God calls you an immigrant, on your way to His country. Live like it.

God, I'm so glad that I have assurance of citizenship
in heaven. Help me live in ways that glorify
You while I'm here. In Jesus' name, amen.

God Calls You a Caregiver

"And the King will answer them, 'Truly, I say to you, as you did it to one of the least of these my brothers, you did it to me.'"
MATTHEW 25:40 ESV

Caregiving is an intense line of work. There are professional caregivers—doctors, nurses, nursing assistants, therapists, and so on. And there are unpaid personal caregivers—parents, spouses, daughters, sons, grandchildren, friends, church families, and more. For those who are "on the clock," caregiving is a job with time limits. For those who are giving out of love, caregiving never ends.

Personal caregivers range from parents of children with special needs to children of parents with dementia. They can be family members of a patient with a terminal illness or friends of a person with a terrifying diagnosis.

At some point in your life, you may be a caregiver for someone in your family or circle of acquaintance. Yet not every action of caregiving is directly associated with a patient in a bed or wheelchair. Some caregiving is in the moment and not stressful; some requires time commitment and physical exertion. If we see someone in need and we are able to assist them, we should do so. Jesus told His listeners that distributing kindness to those who can't help themselves is like a personal service to Him. Imagining Him as the recipient will surely help us keep the right perspective!

Lord, I want to serve You by serving others. Enable me to have patience and kindness and wisdom in how I carry it out. In Jesus' name, amen.

God Calls You to Trust Him in Widowhood

"Let your widows trust in me."
JEREMIAH **49:11** ESV

In the United States, the lifespan of the average woman is five years longer than that of the average man. More women outlive their husbands than the other way around. Because of these statistics, you and I may experience widowhood at some time.

Widowhood is a lonely season. The difficult adjustment to the death of a loved one is often magnified by the growing lack of independence for older women and the loss of social connections and situations once enjoyed as a couple. Some women keep to themselves and withdraw. Others try to reinvent themselves in some way. Most just do the best they can to adapt and enjoy what they still have—health and family and friends.

God knows that being a widow is a difficult season. Scripture references ways the people of God can defend and assist widows. The most important thing we can remember as we realize that widowhood might be in our futures is that God is ever mindful of those who are bereft of protection. He told the prophet that widows can trust Him. If we someday lose our husbands, we may depend on those words.

God calls us to acknowledge His faithfulness in every season. Widowhood is one of them.

Lord, You are Jehovah Tsuri: God Is My Rock.
If I am called to widowhood in some season of life,
I know I can trust You to be there for me. Amen.

God Calls You to Persevere in a Challenging Marriage

Likewise, wives, be subject to your own husbands, so that even if some do not obey the word, they may be won without a word by the conduct of their wives, when they see your respectful and pure conduct.
1 PETER 3:1–2 ESV

Marriage is difficult even in the best of times. It is a lifelong process of blending two lives into one. That takes deliberate, ongoing effort. And in difficult seasons, it is a formidable challenge.

God speaks specifically to wives through the apostle Peter's words. He instructs us to change our husbands through our actions. Though usually it is thought that these words are addressing a situation involving an unbelieving husband, it could also be helpful for the wife whose husband is disobedient to the Word in some other aspect of their relationship. Perhaps he is unintentionally violating the biblical concept of cherishing, sacrificial love. In this instance, God asks her to persevere in her choice to respect him anyway. And she can take her grievances to God. His Spirit can do far more than her words ever could. Of course, there are certainly times when communication is good and necessary. But dependence on God is what scripture recommends.

Heavenly Father, I bring my marriage to You today and ask for Your grace to work in me. Let me know when to speak and when to be silent. Win my husband to truth in Your way. Amen.

God Calls You to Surrender Your Home

*Lord, You have been our dwelling place
and our refuge in all generations.*

PSALM 90:1 AMPC

The American dream includes owning a house. It's considered the foundation of a stable family.

But the ancient Israelites were sometimes nomadic—they lived in tents and makeshift dwellings in certain periods of their history. This was especially true after the exodus from Egypt. At other times, they were settled in the land and built nice homes and planted gardens and vineyards. When Jesus lived on earth, His people, the Jews, had their own land, but it was being occupied by the Romans. And then after the destruction of Jerusalem, the Jews again were dispersed and lived in transit around the world until the formation of the State of Israel in 1948. God truly has been their dwelling place, the stabilization of their people.

Regardless of what we live in, it really belongs to God. It may be a duplex or a condo, a mobile home or a college dorm, a rented house or a family farm. Regardless of the name on the lease or deed, God is the owner. And at some point, He may ask us to offer it back to Him. In those moments, while the flames roar or the tornado howls or the bank demands vacancy and our homes are taken from us, we know that they were only temporary and that God can be trusted.

*O Lord, You are Adonai: Lord God. You are sovereign. You are good.
My home and everything I have belongs to You. You have
called me to surrender it. In Jesus' name, amen.*

God Calls You to Healing

*But Jesus said, Someone did touch Me; for I perceived
that [healing] power has gone forth from Me.*

LUKE 8:46 AMPC

Luke the doctor wrote down the story of Jesus in a little town in Galilee where a woman who had a debilitating disease was determined to be healed. She was so weak that she had difficulty getting to the Master, but she kept going and finally was able to reach her goal—just the hem of His robe. The Bible says that she was healed immediately. Jesus knew it, and she knew it.

Not all of us will be healed. We cannot dictate to the Lord how He should work in our lives. He has a purpose for each of us, and sometimes that is best accomplished by us glorifying Him in the middle of suffering. None of us want that answer, of course, but we must leave the decision with Him.

What we do know for sure is that we can come, just as this nameless woman did, to Jesus. We can ask in prayer. And we know we will receive grace—either healing grace or enduring grace. And one day Jesus will heal us completely in heaven.

*O God, You are Jehovah Rapha: The God Who Heals. I bring to You
my request, and I trust Your answer that is in accordance
with Your purpose in my life. In Jesus' name, amen.*

God Calls You to Amazement

"The very hairs of your head are all numbered."
LUKE 12:7 NKJV

Technology is constantly changing. It is continually advancing. New machines and processes and techniques and inventions amaze us on a daily basis. But nothing will amaze you like this bit of information: God knows how many hairs are on your head. And God holds that information not just on you but on every person living on the globe today. And He has that knowledge about every person who has ever lived! Every single hair at every single moment in every single person's life! That's amazing. That's unfathomable. But that's our God. The Bible says His knowledge is infinite (Psalm 147:5).

Reminding ourselves of the greatness of God's knowledge about us helps us to put our trust in Him. In a culture where many things assault our faith, we need to remind ourselves continually of who God is and what He knows.

In your life today, you may be facing some kind of temptation. Satan wants you to focus on your little world and forget about the bigness of the One who created You. Remember today that God wants you to be amazed by His love and that He calls you to stand back in His presence and let Him awe you with the knowledge He has of you.

Heavenly Father, thank You for Your astounding knowledge of me. I ask You to help me focus on You and live my life in Your presence. In Jesus' name, amen.

Chosen for Seasons
God Calls You to Live and Die

For everything there is a season, and a time for every matter
under heaven: a time to be born, and a time to die.
ECCLESIASTES 3:1–2 ESV

Your life is not a random act of matter. It is a planned event. It is a calling, a sacred trust. God brought you into being, and He has a time for your life to end. The acceptance of these facts is the basis of peace in your life.

In the beginning of our world, God created the seasons. Genesis 1:14 tells us that God created the seasons. In Genesis 8:22 God promised Noah and his descendants that the seasons would never stop cycling through as long as the earth remains. He gave us the seasons not only for beauty and variety but also for the growth of vegetation and nature and for the life cycles of the animals. He has a purpose for it all.

The writer of Ecclesiastes uses the analogy of seasons to teach us about the various time frames of our lives. Often we can better understand what is happening to us spiritually through our understanding of what is happening in the world around us.

So the verses in this chapter remind us that there are times for every single event and every single adjustment we face. And the most basic fact of all is a time for birth and a time for death. As we trust Him with this and with what goes in between, we can live our lives in ways that bring Him glory.

Father, thank You for appointing the time for me
to be born and a time for me to die. I will trust
You with what comes in between. Amen.

God Calls You to Plant and Reap

A time to plant, and a time to pluck up what is planted.
ECCLESIASTES 3:2 ESV

In the spring, farmers begin to plow their fields to prepare them for planting. Dirt clods must be broken up and the furrows made soft to receive the seeds. Then, after the fields are planted, the farmers wait for rain to moisten the earth and begin the decaying process in the seed. And as the death takes place, new life springs forth from it and a tiny green shoot pushes up through the sod. Then the growing season begins and the plant becomes strong and vibrant, producing fruit. When the harvest comes, the pickers or the machines pluck from the earth the ripened product of the seed. And the harvest nourishes the world.

You and I experience seasons of planting, times when God allows our emotional and spiritual fields to be prepared and precious seeds to be dropped into the furrows of our hearts. As we soak our minds in the rain of God's Word and in prayer, the seed begins to open up and produce a sprout of new life. Before long a new spiritual habit or discipline has taken root in us and is producing fruit. And then God starts the process again in another area. Someday when we are fully mature, God will pluck up what He has planted and transplant us into a better place where our fruit will be seen.

You are called to submit to God's planting and growing process.

Lord God, I am ready for You to start preparing me for growth.
You are the Master Gardener, and I trust You. Amen.

God Calls You to Understand Life

A time to kill, and a time to heal.
ECCLESIASTES 3:3 ESV

The wise writer of Ecclesiastes tells us that there is a time for wounding, even killing, and there is a time for healing. Immediately the sixth of the Ten Commandments comes to mind: "Thou shalt not kill" (Exodus 20:13 KJV). We understand that God is telling us not to intentionally take a human life. He created that life; it is His to give and His to take.

But the deeper truth at work here is that God is in charge of all the aspects of our world, and at times He allows consequences to take their natural course. This verse could have particular reference to military conflicts or to the just execution of criminals. There are times when the most proper thing a country or government can do is take life because, in doing so, it is preserving other lives.

But then the writer reminds us that there is also a time to heal. God ordains those who have gifts in healing. He allows earthly physicians to be ministers of healing and comfort. The Hebrew word used in this verse carries with it the idea of using a needle to sew. It reminds us of the prophecy about Jesus in Isaiah 61:1 (ESV) that He will "bind up the brokenhearted." The meaning here can also refer to the healing of national hurts.

God calls us to understand life from His perspective. Life is given and life is taken. And He is the source of it all.

Lord God, You are the originator of human life.
Help me to honor it in all its forms and be Your
minister of healing at the right time. Amen.

God Calls You to Be an Engineer

A time to break down, and a time to build up.
ECCLESIASTES 3:3 ESV

Watching classic neighborhoods being destroyed so that institutional-type condos and apartments can be built may make us sad. But observing dumpy, run-down city districts being razed to be turned into beautiful parks or other worthy spaces for the community can be exhilarating. The difference is in why and how the tearing down is done.

The idea in this verse is that there are times when something needs to be "broken down." It can mean to breach, as in finally getting through to the goal, and it can mean to apply pressure, as in cajoling someone until he or she changes their mind. Often in our relationships with others, there is a need to breach, to break through a wall that has built up between us. We need to know how to demolish those barriers and do it skillfully and prayerfully.

Then equally important is that we understand when and how to build up and establish and make something permanent. As followers of Christ, we recognize the value of a solid foundation for our lives and our relationships. Psalm 127:1 (ESV) tells us, "Unless the LORD builds the house, those who build it labor in vain." His principles are the ones on which we can build something that will last. He calls us to this ministry of breaking down and building.

Lord, teach me to know when to breach a barrier and when to lay a foundation. I want to honor You in my relationships. In Jesus' name, amen.

God Calls You to Know How to Respond

A time to weep, and a time to laugh.
ECCLESIASTES 3:4 ESV

Laughter is healthy, scientists and doctors tell us. But God always knew that. He created us with the ability to make laughter, a physical response to humor. This expulsion of air and sound accompanied by gestures varies with each individual and is extremely healthy for the body and brain. In fact, laughter involves both sides of the brain as well as the frontal lobe, limbic system, and motor areas. All in all, laughter creates happiness throughout our beings; it helps us adapt to awkward situations, relieves stress, and even boosts the immune system. Human beings are the only species that have proved to have a direct laugh response. God said it was very good. And Proverbs 17:22 reminds us that a merry or joyful heart is like good medicine. We can use this gift of laughter to encourage others.

But our Creator also wants us to know how to grieve when it is appropriate. If we realize the somberness of life, we can then celebrate all the more fully at the other times. As a nation of people, it is right and good for us to weep over our collective guilt from atrocities like abortion, sexual wantonness, arrogance, rebellion, and the removal of God from society. This is the distinction to which we are called.

Creator God, You designed us with the ability both to weep and to laugh. Today, help me to know the proper time for both. Amen.

God Calls You to Know When to Celebrate

A time to mourn, and a time to dance.

ECCLESIASTES 3:4 ESV

God wants us to know how and when to celebrate. The Bible makes frequent mention of feast days and celebrations. God instituted national feast days in the Old Testament (Leviticus 23) and even a special celebration called the Year of Jubilee when debts were canceled, slaves and prisoners were freed, and the land was allowed to rest (Leviticus 25). Jesus told a parable about two sons and how the father threw a celebration when the prodigal returned home; He likened that to the celebration in heaven when a sinner is saved (Luke 15). The apostle Paul tells us about a great celebration that will take place in heaven someday—the marriage supper of the Lamb (Revelation 19:9).

But God also tells us that there is a time to mourn. In fact, Ecclesiastes 7:2 (KJV) says that "it is better to go to the house of mourning, than to go to the house of feasting." There are times when a sober approach to life circumstances is needed. It is right and good to mourn over sin and its effect on others. We cannot ignore the terrible consequences of rebellion against God. It is fitting to mourn death. Jacob mourned when he presumed his son Joseph had been killed (Genesis 37:34). The Israelites mourned the death of Moses (Deuteronomy 34:8) and Aaron (Numbers 20:29). The early church mourned over the first martyr, Stephen (Acts 8:2). When we mourn death, we recognize the awful result of sin at work in our world and we agree with God that we were made, not to die, but to live forever with Him.

Life is a variety of situations and seasons, and God calls you to approach each with knowledge.

Almighty God, thank You for ruling over the affairs of this world. Whether I face feasting or mourning today, give me the grace to do it well. In Jesus' name, amen.

61

God Calls You to Discernment

*A time to cast away stones, and a time
to gather stones together.*
ECCLESIASTES 3:5 ESV

At times in our lives, we need to fling stones away from us. The stones in your experience may be old hurts or childhood trauma or church conflicts or relational baggage. Whatever it is, there comes a time to get rid of it.

In Hebrews 12:1 (ESV), the writer exhorts us to "lay aside every weight" that hinders our spiritual race. Runners wear light clothing and specially designed shoes. They do not carry extra baggage. Neither can we in a spiritual sense. Satan wants to use the past against us. Christ calls us to forgive those who have wronged us and find the power in Him to deal with traumatic memories. We can live in the present by His grace.

But there is also a time to gather stones together. Joshua commanded the people of Israel to build a memorial of twelve stones representing the twelve Hebrew tribes after they had miraculously crossed the Jordan River (Joshua 4:1–9). This would be a reminder to them and to their children and grandchildren of the power of God.

You need to build spiritual memorials in your life. Maybe you can do this by noting in your journal when God answers a specific need or when He changes your heart with His power. Gathering stones together can be a spiritual benefit to us all.

*Lord God, give me the discernment to know when to gather
stones and when to release them. Let every monument
in my life be one that brings glory to You. Amen.*

God Calls You to Cherish the Right Things

A time to embrace, and a time to refrain from embracing.
ECCLESIASTES 3:5 ESV

God created us with a need for closeness, for relationship, for intimacy. He intends for us to be fulfilled through interaction with other human beings, in both casual and covenant ways. We can derive satisfaction from friendships, but our deeper emotional needs are met through marriage and family. All of us need a few people in our lives to whom we can cling in every season of life. These are the people we embrace both literally and figuratively. We hold them dear. They are gifts.

God also gives us earthly possessions. He has provided the materials on earth that inventors and crafters use to build and engineer and design. We may embrace these in one sense of the word while always keeping in mind that people are worth more than stuff.

But there are also times when we must relinquish our hold on people and on possessions. We all will have times when we realize that God gives and takes, and that only He is the one thing we can't do without.

The Old Testament figure Job had this moment. After his estate and his livestock and his children were all taken from him in the space of one day, Job fell to the ground in grief and surrender and worshipped. He said, "The LORD gave, and the LORD hath taken away; blessed be the name of the LORD" (Job 1:21 KJV).

Job knew what to embrace and when to refrain from embracing. He knew the One from whom all things flow. God calls us to know that too.

Father in heaven, You have given me many good things,
both people and possessions. Help me to know when to embrace
them and when to relinquish them. In Jesus' name, amen.

God Calls You to Look for What Lasts

A time to seek, and a time to lose.
ECCLESIASTES 3:6 ESV

In Luke 15 Jesus told parables about lost things. A woman lost a gold piece and searched her whole house until she found it. A man lost a sheep, and he left ninety-nine in the sheepfold and went looking in rough terrain until he could rescue the one. And a father never stopped hoping and watching for the return of his youngest son who was lost to the family.

In another parable, Jesus related how a man found a treasure in a field and then set about liquidating his other assets so that he could purchase the one thing that had more value (Matthew 13:44). In this way, we are to seek salvation and relationship with Jesus. We are to value that above any other discovery we might make. Our souls are worth more than any other treasure. Jesus asked His listeners, "For what will it profit a man if he gains the whole world and forfeits his soul? Or what shall a man give in return for his soul?" (Matthew 16:26 ESV).

Likewise, there are things we can lose that allow us to gain other things. Paul wrote to his fellow Christians, "But whatever gain I had, I counted as loss for the sake of Christ. Indeed, I count everything as loss because of the surpassing worth of knowing Christ Jesus my Lord. For his sake I have suffered the loss of all things and count them as rubbish, in order that I may gain Christ" (Philippians 3:7–8 ESV).

As a Christ follower, you are called to find what lasts. Start that today.

*Lord, today I want to spend my time looking
for what lasts in Your kingdom. Amen.*

God Calls You to Spiritual Tending

A time to keep, and a time to cast away.

ECCLESIASTES 3:6 ESV

Keeping or "tending" a garden has become fashionable. The nutritional value placed on organic fruits and vegetables has increased the desire to have a garden patch, whether in the backyard of a country home or in a raised bed in the city.

The wisdom writer expresses this idea in Ecclesiastes 3:6. The original word for "keep" here meant to tend or guard, to preserve and protect. Gardeners are very familiar with that concept because any plot of ground left to itself is soon overrun with weeds and briars. A garden is a place where intentional care is taken to keep rogue nature at bay so that beautiful nature can bloom.

In our Christian lives, we need to be kept and preserved. We face many dangers to our spiritual selves that can choke the life of God out of our hearts. Jesus referred to this in His parable of the sower and the seed when He said, "The cares of the world and the deceitfulness of riches and the desires for other things enter in and choke the word, and it proves unfruitful" (Mark 4:19 ESV). You and I must be aware of the dangers and rely on God's strength for protection. David wrote in Psalm 121:5 (ESV), "The LORD is your keeper." We can rely on Him.

Of course, we must also recognize when it is wise for us to cast something away. The apostle Paul wrote to his young protégé Timothy, "Flee youthful passions and pursue righteousness, faith, love, and peace, along with those who call on the Lord from a pure heart" (2 Timothy 2:22 ESV).

God calls you and me to tend our spiritual selves by knowing when to keep and when to cast away.

*Father, help me to recognize what I need to cast away
and what I need to preserve. In Jesus' name, amen.*

God Calls You to
Care for the Seams

A time to tear, and a time to sew.
ECCLESIASTES 3:7 ESV

I am not a seamstress. Regrettably so since both my maternal grand-mother and my mother were amazing ones. But one thing I do know is that when you are finished with a seam, you must reinforce it with a few extra stitches. This secures what you have done so that it doesn't rip out.

Ecclesiastes 3:7 speaks of there being a time to tear out a seam, and every good seamstress knows that there is a time when something must be ripped out. Unfortunately for me, I have become very well acquainted with that trusty little tool, the stitch ripper. Sometimes the seam isn't right or it's in the wrong place, or something else is wrong, but ripping it out must take place for the piece to be right.

The Hebrew word here is *qāra'*, and it carries the meaning of "to rend." This is a common phrase in scripture, and it is usually found in a passage where someone is rending his or her garments in sorrow, either in mourning over a tragedy or in repentance for sin. To have a proper relationship with God, we must know when to rip out of our lives those things that are wrong. If something is done improperly, the finished product won't be right no matter how great the other seams are.

We are called to tear out the bad and anchor the good.

Father, thank You for giving us the natural world, which You use to illustrate spiritual truths. Help me to know when to secure the seam and when to rip it out. Amen.

God Calls You to Rule Your Tongue

A time to keep silence, and a time to speak.
ECCLESIASTES 3:7 ESV

Perhaps the most difficult discipline to learn is the discipline of the tongue. In the New Testament book of James, the writer remarks how we can build rudders to steer ships and put bits in horses' mouths to steer them, but we can't seem to make something that controls the tongue (James 3). He says that if a person can control his or her tongue, they can master any other part of the body (James 3:2).

We see this example in the life of Jesus, who exercised perfect control over His body, though He was living with temptation in the same way we are. Many times He was verbally attacked and maligned by the scribes and Pharisees, and instead of retorting in a vengeful way, He chose words of truth or said nothing at all. When He was on trial before Pilate, Jesus chose not to answer every question (Matthew 26:63). He did not defend Himself in such a way that would have stopped the execution process; He knew He had to go to the cross to complete our redemption. The prophet Isaiah predicted this: "Like a sheep that before its shearers is silent, so he opened not his mouth" (Isaiah 53:7 ESV). The apostle Peter repeated it in his letter: "When he was reviled, he did not revile in return; when he suffered, he did not threaten" (1 Peter 2:23 ESV). Probably nothing will more greatly reveal the power of the Holy Spirit at work in us than our ability through Christ to control our words.

Lord Jesus, You are the perfect example of using the gift of words well. Give me grace today to be like You. Amen.

God Calls You to Love Him Best

A time to love, and a time to hate.
ECCLESIASTES 3:8 ESV

Love is one emotion that receives a lot of attention in our human world. We were created with a need to be loved and to love in return. This passage is clear that there is an appropriate time to love. And the original wording even suggests that it is an intense love, one that is connected to breathing, like a vital part of life. It is used of Abraham loving his son Isaac whom God asked Abraham to sacrifice as an offering (Genesis 22:2). It is used in Deuteronomy 6:5 to tell us to love God with all our hearts, souls, and might. It is a right and proper emotion when surrendered to the lordship of Christ.

But there may come a time when we have to turn from something almost as though we hate it. If a person or a hobby or a possession has become an idol in our lives, taking up more space in our hearts and thoughts than God, we are called to turn away from it. We must regard it as an enemy of the life of God within us. We are called to love Him best.

Holy God, You gave us the gift of love and then showed us how to use it through Your Son. Today I ask You to help me hold the dear things in my life in proper balance. In Jesus' name, amen.

God Calls You to Choose the Winning Side

A time for war, and a time for peace.
ECCLESIASTES 3:8 ESV

Wars are part of human history. They are actually necessary in our fallen world for the battle against unrighteousness. The first war ever was started by Satan when he revolted against God (Isaiah 14:13–14). He wanted to ascend to God's throne and rule, to be above the Creator. But he was cast out of heaven, and with him were cast out the angels who joined in his rebellion (2 Peter 2:4). A war with God will never be won by anyone, human or angelic, but prophecy tells us that Satan will try again in the last days. "I saw the beast and the kings of the earth with their armies gathered to make war against him who was sitting on the horse and against his army" (Revelation 19:19 ESV).

But the One on that white horse is Jesus: "The one sitting on it is called Faithful and True, and in righteousness he judges and makes war" (Revelation 19:11 ESV). The righteous warrior Jesus is also the Prince of Peace. When the eternal victory is won, He will bring peace to our world like we have never known. Today He calls us to choose the winning side so that we can be with Him forever.

Lord Jesus, I look forward to the day when You arrive on a white horse to conquer and to reign. I choose Your side today! Amen.

Chosen for Christlikeness

Chosen at the Cross

For the word of the cross is folly to those who are perishing,
but to us who are being saved it is the power of God.
1 CORINTHIANS 1:18 ESV

Jesus chose to bear the cross for your sake. He chose to die on the cross for your salvation.

In the days of the Roman Empire, there was no more painful or humiliating death than that of the cross. It was reserved for the vilest offenders, the worst criminals, the dregs of society that the government wished to use as examples. If one's relative was crucified, it was a public shame, something one did not talk about. It was associated with embarrassment and criminality. So, for the disciples of Jesus to find glory in the cross was puzzling to the rest of the world. They could see nothing wonderful about such a death. But they missed the fact that Jesus chose to be humiliated and tortured and executed for us! Because we deserved that kind of death, He had to experience it. He could not bypass the pain or the shame. In those horrible moments, He chose you and me.

No wonder the apostle Paul could write, "Far be it from me to boast except in the cross of our Lord Jesus Christ, by which the world has been crucified to me, and I to the world" (Galatians 6:14 ESV).

Jesus, thank You for taking my place on the cross. I glory in that.
You paid for my redemption. Thank You for choosing me. Amen.

Chosen in the Resurrection

If we have died with Christ,
we believe that we will also live with him.

ROMANS 6:8 ESV

God created us as eternal beings. When Adam and Eve sinned and death entered our world, it affected both our physical bodies and our spiritual selves. Without the redeeming work of Jesus, we have no hope of anything but eternal death—in body and in spirit. But because He conquered sin on the cross and triumphed over death in His resurrection, we too can live forever.

He offers us spiritual life as we believe on Him for salvation. And when we do, we are assured of physical life forever when this present body dies. It will be transformed into a new body at the resurrection of the saints.

This is the best possible news any of us can have. We are not doomed. We have hope. Death is the worst enemy we have on earth. As mothers, we fear the specter of death in the lives of our children—we anxiously check their breathing when they're infants; we take them to well checks when they're children; we ask them to let us know when they arrive safely at a destination when they're in college. We know that death hovers over our world, ready to snatch another victim.

But death is defeated in the eternal sense because Jesus chose us. Today you can go out and face your life armed with that assurance.

Lord Jesus, I am so glad You conquered death for me.
Thank You for eternal life in my body and spirit. Amen.

Chosen for Surrender

*With eyes wide open to the mercies of God, I beg
you, my brothers, as an act of intelligent worship,
to give him your bodies, as a living sacrifice,
consecrated to him and acceptable by him.*
ROMANS 12:1 PHILLIPS

The offering of sacrifices was common in the Old Testament. God instituted this as a way of looking forward to the perfect sacrifice of Jesus, the Lamb of God. As the people selected the best lamb in their flock and let its life be spilled on the altar, they were reminded in vivid color of the price of sin and of the need for a messiah.

Jesus' sacrifice was sufficient for the sins of the whole world. There is no more need for sacrifices at an earthly temple. What we are asked to do now is to offer ourselves as living sacrifices. After we have been saved by the power of God, we are admonished by the inspired writer of Romans to climb up on the altar of sacrifice and surrender our everyday lives to His use. He does not want us to be dead sacrifices, but living ones, lives ready to take action when He calls.

You were chosen for surrender. Satan wants you to believe that doing things your own way is the pathway to fulfillment. But he is the father of lies (John 8:44).

God offers us the joy of surrender; it is our "act of intelligent worship."

*Dear Father, I present myself to You. On this altar of surrender,
I give You all I am and ask You to use me for Your purpose. Amen.*

Chosen for Understanding

Your hands have made me and fashioned me; give me understanding, that I may learn Your commandments.
PSALM 119:73 NKJV

We live in a world where there is a continuous flow of information. Not only do we have national and global news at our fingertips, but we also have a vast database of knowledge about everything from history to trivia to recipes available anytime, night or day. We are a very informed, educated society.

But there is a difference in being informed and in knowing how to use that information. When the psalmist lived, there were no resources like the ones we have today, but there were great teachers and there was knowledge to be gained. Yet he realized that understanding was vital if one is to know how to live life.

The meaning of understanding here is perception, discernment, the ability to distinguish how to use one's knowledge. It is an important trait for anyone who wants to live life well, and especially so for one who is following Christ. You will encounter many people who have knowledge about life, but if they do not know the purpose of their own lives or understand that God is the center of all existence, they will flounder in some area of their lives. As followers of Jesus, we have been chosen for understanding. And we may ask Him for it today.

Dear Lord, I want to live my life with godly understanding. I ask You for that today. Amen.

Chosen for a Good Name

A good name is to be chosen rather than great riches,
loving favor rather than silver and gold.

PROVERBS 22:1 NKJV

Do you like your first name? Many people don't. For whatever reason, many of us don't care for the name our parents so carefully selected for us. We may prefer a friend's name or a name we hear in a store or see on a list somewhere. And though we have even less control over it, some of us dislike our last names too.

Unless we go through the legal process to change our names, we have to submit to our parents' prerogative and accept the name we have been given. It becomes our identity.

The wisdom writer tells us that we can choose a good name. Oh, maybe not the actual name itself, but the reputation behind it. When someone hears your name, he or she will have an immediate emotional reaction. As Christ followers, we strive to make that a positive one.

And there is no better name we can choose for ourselves than Christian—one who is like Christ. That is the best name of all. We can choose it because He first chose us.

Heavenly Father, thank You for choosing me to be like Jesus
and for wanting to give me His name. Help me
honor it in the way I live. Amen.

Chosen for Health

Be not wise in your own eyes; fear the LORD, and turn away from evil. It will be healing to your flesh and refreshment to your bones.

PROVERBS 3:7–8 ESV

Traditional medicine and alternative healing are often at odds with each other since they tend to value different approaches. Whereas traditional medical wisdom seeks to use procedures and pharmaceuticals in intervention, naturalists seek to guide the body to heal itself through the use of herbs and supplements. Both have their place. And some physicians are increasingly using both kinds of treatments.

Some righteous people in the Bible suffered. And Jesus did not heal every sick person on earth while He walked here. In fact, He told his disciples that some suffering that people endure is so that the glory of God can be seen in them (John 9:3).

We know that illness is part of human existence in our fallen world. But there are actually some health benefits of turning from evil and honoring the Lord. Such a person would stay away from substances that are harmful to the body, would have more peace of mind and thus suffer less from the effects of stress, and would engage in healthy moral behaviors and practices that would prevent certain types of diseases and situations.

You are chosen to experience health. And following God's Word can help you do that.

Lord, You are the Maker of my body, and You know how it works. Help me honor Your design by following a healthy, biblical lifestyle. In Jesus' name, amen.

Chosen to Build Others Up

Let no corrupting talk come out of your mouths,
but only such as is good for building up, as fits the
occasion, that it may give grace to those who hear.
EPHESIANS 4:29 ESV

Social media is a wonderful platform for interaction, but it does bring certain challenges with it. As the public forum of our day, it is a place where ideas are brought to the table but also the place where opinions are expressed and passions are aired. This is fine as long as we are mature enough to handle it. But frequently commenters are either immature or have a sarcastic temperament, and the words they post start a firestorm. Others pile onto the discussion, either defending their friend or adding fuel to the dissention. And if we are not careful, harm is done to relationships.

Some choose to counteract this damage by withdrawing from the forum entirely or by relegating their posts to memes of puppy dogs and recipes for delicious desserts. That might be helpful for some, but ignoring the reality of varying viewpoints will not make them go away.

We need to learn to build others up even in a disagreement. We can choose words and phrasing patterns and punctuation that de-escalate the animosity and place value on the people involved. Winning a debate at the cost of friendship is too high a price.

You are chosen to build others up. And that includes social media!

Lord, use my words today to minister grace to those
who hear or read them. In Jesus' name, amen.

Chosen to Show Hospitality

Show hospitality to one another without grumbling.
1 Peter 4:9 esv

I like the first word of this verse. It's an action word, a decisive word. That's how we need to practice hospitality—deliberately. God, knowing all things and knowing how we work, inspired the apostle Peter to tell us just to go ahead and act in hospitable ways whether we feel like it or not.

Hospitality is a way to show Christlikeness to those around us. After all, Jesus went to great personal cost to show kindness to us. That is the core of hospitality—sharing what you have with others, even if it costs you, even if it's inconvenient, even if they don't deserve it.

In New Testament times, it was vital that the believers were hospitable to one another. There was widespread persecution of Christians; many had lost their homes and businesses, and some were in transition. Many uprooted their families and moved to another place to escape death or imprisonment. They needed to be received and helped by the churches in their area.

We may not face the same kind of dangers today, but we do need to open our homes and hearts to one another. Satan will try to destroy our church families, but being together helps us guard against that.

You are called to show hospitality.

Lord, You let Yourself be inconvenienced for me;
help me to do that for others. Amen.

Chosen for Victory

The Lord knows how to deliver the godly out of temptations.
2 Peter 2:9 NKJV

Some Christian songs focus on struggle, on the difficulty of temptation, and on the concept of trying again after failure. And while it is true that we must have a resilience founded in the redeeming love of Jesus, it is also true that we can experience victory over temptation.

We need balance. It would not be right to glamorize the Christian life until it appears that there are no hard places in the path. It doesn't take very long for a new believer to figure out the truth! But it is also not right to make it appear that victory is only for super saints. Jesus died a cruel death on a cross so that we could have power over sin. If we do not believe that is possible, we are saying that His death is ineffectual.

We can live in victory because Jesus won it for us. Scripture tells us that Christ triumphed over sin and death and took their keys from Satan. "I am He who lives, and was dead, and behold, I am alive forevermore. Amen. And I have the keys of Hades and of Death" (Revelation 1:18 NKJV).

We are to imitate our Lord. We are to seek victory over the temptations in our lives. In those areas where we are vulnerable, we need to pray for strength and then do something practical about it like setting boundaries and having a friend hold us accountable.

We are chosen for victory. And it is possible.

*Lord Jesus, thank You for winning the victory and
for enabling me to be victorious also. Amen.*

Chosen to Be Cleansed

But you were washed, but you were sanctified,
but you were justified in the name of the
Lord Jesus and by the Spirit of our God.
1 CORINTHIANS 6:11 NKJV

Leprosy was a plague in ancient times. The diagnosis was quite literally a death sentence—a physical death as well as a social, relational, and emotional one. A person with leprosy would be made to leave his or her home and family and take up residence in a leper colony, which was often close to the city dump. There the miserable souls would try to care for and comfort one another as the disease progressed and they lost digits and limbs and eyesight and hearing and finally succumbed in death.

In scripture, leprosy is sometimes symbolic of the decay of sin. But Jesus brings cleansing from sin just as a person cured of leprosy was considered clean and could return to normal life. One first needed to show himself to the priest for his cleansing to be verified. "It happened when He was in a certain city, that behold, a man who was full of leprosy saw Jesus; and he fell on his face and implored Him, saying, 'Lord, if You are willing, You can make me clean.' Then He put out His hand and touched him, saying, 'I am willing; be cleansed.' Immediately the leprosy left him" (Luke 5:12–13 NKJV). Likewise, Jesus brings cleansing to the soul that is decaying with sin. One touch of His mercy upon us and we are washed clean.

Jesus, I revel in Your cleansing power.
Thank You for making me clean. Amen.

Chosen for Suffering

*For to this you were called, because Christ also suffered for us,
leaving us an example, that you should follow His steps.*
1 PETER 2:21 NKJV

Being chosen for suffering doesn't sound like the invitation that most of us want. In fact, we do everything we can to avoid suffering. And we should. A person who wants to experience pain usually has some sort of psychological issue. But suffering is one of the tools God uses to chip away at the rough edges of our lives and make us more like Jesus. Obviously, we experience suffering for a different reason than He did. He was the perfect Son of God; we have much imperfection. But scripture does tell us something very interesting in Hebrews 5:8 (NKJV): "Though He was a Son, yet He learned obedience by the things which He suffered."

Though Christ was never disobedient, He put into practice on earth what was never questioned—doing the will of the Father. And if He needed to practice obedience by suffering, so do we.

Some believers endure intense physical suffering because of disease. Others endure emotional and relational suffering. Still others are tested in difficult ministry situations. And of course, there are believers around the world who are being persecuted and tortured and martyred for their faith. In all these instances, their suffering is not in vain. The Christ who suffered for them keeps track of their days and nights. And He will sustain them.

*Father God, You have chosen for me to be like Jesus
in suffering. I accept Your will for me. Amen.*

Chosen for Good Works

For we are His workmanship, created in Christ Jesus for
good works, which God prepared beforehand
that we should walk in them.
Ephesians 2:10 nkjv

Because we are saved by faith alone and not by works, some Christians have the idea that works are not really important. They are wrong. What we do cannot save us, but what we do reflects who our Father is.

Jesus told His listeners to the Sermon on the Mount, "Let your light so shine before men, that they may see your good works and glorify your Father in heaven" (Matthew 5:16 nkjv).

The apostle Paul reminded the church at Ephesus that they were created "for" good works that God had prepared for them to do.

In doing good works, we can be like Jesus. Acts 10:38 (nkjv) records that "God anointed Jesus of Nazareth with the Holy Spirit and with power, who went about doing good."

All of these are very good reasons for us to be intentional and purposeful about doing good for others. What can you do today? Maybe something extra or unexpected. The world calls that doing "random acts of kindness." God calls it being like Jesus.

Dear God, open my eyes today to see the ways in which I can
reflect Jesus and bring You glory through doing good. Amen.

Chosen for Redemption

*In him we have redemption through his blood, the forgiveness
of our trespasses, according to the riches of his grace.*
Ephesians 1:7 esv

The word *redemption* is one of the most beautiful in the Bible. And it is illustrated over and over again in the stories within it.

To be redeemed is to be made anew, to have the flaws fixed, to be given another chance. This is the core of what God did for all humanity through Jesus.

In the garden, after man and woman sinned, God found a way to reconcile them to Himself. He didn't want to destroy them because of their sin, but in His holiness, He could not have fellowship with them. So He purposed that a perfect Redeemer would pay for their sin and become the living bridge back to God. Revelation 13:8 (nkjv) says that Jesus, the Lamb, was "slain from the foundation of the world." God, knowing all things, had a plan in place from eternity past. There was never a question if God would redeem us. He had already chosen that. Our redemption is settled according to the riches of His grace.

*Heavenly Father, thank You for planning and carrying
out Your plan of redemption for me. I love You and
offer my redeemed life back to You. Amen.*

Chosen for Scars

I bear on my body the marks of Jesus.
GALATIANS 6:17 ESV

Then [Jesus] said to Thomas, "Put your finger here,
and see my hands; and put out your hand, and place
it in my side. Do not disbelieve, but believe."
JOHN 20:27 ESV

Babies are usually born fresh and sweet, free from scars. They have not yet lived in the outside world nor acquired the marks and spots that show where mishaps have taken place. But as children grow, they experience bruises and gashes, broken limbs and other effects of falling and tripping and discovering the world in active ways. And as adults, we receive scars from medical procedures as well as from a few humbling clumsy moments or perhaps from more serious accidents. Scars are the testament to living life.

Jesus bears scars. After His resurrection, in His risen body, he retained the nail marks in His hands and feet and the scar from the sword piercing His side. He bears the scars of our redemption.

You and I are also chosen for scars. We will not have any that will compare to those of Christ, but we will bear in our souls and perhaps our bodies the reminders that we have chosen to serve Him. Paul wrote these words to Timothy: "Indeed, all who desire to live a godly life in Christ Jesus will be persecuted" (2 Timothy 3:12 ESV).

Someday, when we get to heaven, our scars will be gone, but Christ's will remain.

Lord Jesus, thank You for bearing scars for me.
I am so glad You went all the way to the cross
and didn't back away. I love You. Amen.

Chosen for Honor

Chosen for Faithful Living

I have chosen the way of faithfulness;
I set your rules before me.
PSALM 119:30 ESV

God has chosen us to live lives of honor, but to make that happen, you and I must choose also. We must choose to be faithful, that is, to take action to make living a life of honor a reality. Faithfulness doesn't happen in the figurative realm. Faithfulness is acting out in good and responsible and godly ways all the time every day, week after week, month after month, year after year.

Living a faithful life sounds overwhelming when one thinks of all the minutes involved in those years and all the decisions and choices that are part of the dynamic of life. But God doesn't want us to focus on the tedium, the possibility of failure, or the crushing pressure to get everything right. He wants us to focus on this moment, this event, this decision. When we have done it correctly, we can move on to the next one. And just as His grace is available now, it will be available then. He will help us in that moment too.

Satan wants to keep that truth from us. He tells us that we will mess up in all those unknown minutes to come. But he doesn't tell the truth. And the Father gently reminds us through His Holy Spirit to keep making progress and rest in the fact that He will be there.

You are chosen for faithfulness. Choose to act on it this minute.

Dear God, give me today the grace I need to choose
rightly and act decisively. In Jesus' name, amen.

Chosen for Riches

*Listen, my beloved brothers, has not God chosen those who are
poor in the world to be rich in faith and heirs of the kingdom,
which he has promised to those who love him?*
JAMES 2:5 ESV

The Bible tells us that Christians are chosen for riches, but they are a
different kind than those for which the world clamors. We are chosen
to be rich in faith, to be heirs of the kingdom.

Jesus often taught about the kingdom of heaven. And in this realm
of holiness and right, things are different than in the world. The values
by which the kingdom of heaven operates are countercultural down
here. The goals on which it thrives are rubbish on earth. The principles
that guide the lives of its citizens are backward to everything taught
in worldly wisdom. But the kingdom of heaven is the true kingdom,
the everlasting kingdom.

Hebrews 11:6 declares that it is impossible to please God without
faith—faith in His existence and His character. Furthermore, we can't
even conjure up this faith on our own! We can only exercise this kind
of faith because of the witness of nature and our own consciences
that there is a God. Then we begin to build on that foundation through
obedience, and the riches of our faith begin to increase.

You are chosen to be rich in faith. Start where you are and keep
building!

*Dear Lord, I want my faith in You to grow and produce results
so that I can be a millionaire in faith points! Amen.*

Chosen for Delight

Those of crooked heart are an abomination to the LORD,
but those of blameless ways are his delight.
PROVERBS 11:20 ESV

Delight is one of those words that sounds like ice cream on a hot afternoon. It just has a pleasant ring to it.

We are told in scripture to delight ourselves in the Lord, but here is another angle: God delights in those whose ways are blameless. Of course, none of us can be blameless on our own, so this means that the only way to achieve it is through a relationship with Him. And now you see the full circle—if we are in a relationship with God, we can have victory over the temptations Satan brings, and that delights our Father's heart.

The apostle Peter wrote under the inspiration of the Holy Spirit that believers are "partakers of the divine nature, having escaped the corruption that is in the world through lust" (2 Peter 1:4 KJV). That sure sounds like victory and living a blameless life.

For someone to take delight in us is a high compliment; it draws us to them. We feel significant. When God delights in us, it isn't because He admires us but because He finds joy in relationship with us. His grace makes that possible. And that's the best way to happiness for us too.

Dear Father, I want You to be able to delight in me. Guide me
into a deeper relationship with You. In Jesus' name, amen.

Chosen for Worship

*Exalt the L*ORD *our God, and worship at his*
*holy mountain; for the L*ORD *our God is holy!*
PSALM 99:9 ESV

"True worshipers will worship the Father in spirit and truth,
for the Father is seeking such people to worship him."
JOHN 4:23 ESV

In our human minds, commanding another to worship you is an act of egotism. But in the heavenly realm, the command of God for us to worship Him is the only right thing for Him to do. There is no being or entity higher than God; no other to whom ultimate praise should go. For Him *not* to command us to worship Him would be evil; God must be truthful, for that is His character.

I heard someone say once that envy is wanting what belongs to someone else, but jealousy is wanting what is rightfully mine. This would be true in the example of appropriate jealousy between a husband and wife. It is not wrong for either of them to expect the other to spend more of their free time with them than someone else—that is what is rightfully theirs. And the same is true of God. He says He is a jealous God not in a way that is petulant and narcissistic but in a holy way that recognizes what is truth and what is right.

We are only happy when God is at the center of our lives, because we were made to worship. We were chosen for it.

God, I want to worship You in the way that is right.
Thank You for calling me into relationship with You. Amen.

Chosen for Promises
Chosen for Protection

"The LORD will fight for you, and you have only to be silent."
EXODUS 14:14 ESV

There is perhaps nothing more endearing to a young woman than a young man's willingness to fight for her. For him to stand up on her behalf opens her heart like nothing else. Many of the great fairy tales have this angle built into the plot—a beautiful maiden is harassed by a nasty villain, and a handsome hero does battle for her. This story line always speaks to us because it is the plot of redemption played over and over in earthly tales. Jesus is the champion who came from heaven to defeat the enemy and win His bride, the Church. The awe of that is written into our DNA.

The words of Exodus 14:14 were spoken by Moses to the Israelites as they faced another battle with their enemies. They had been tramping through the land of Canaan, facing hostile groups one after another. They were not an organized military power when they left Egypt; they were a nation of people with families, an elderly population, and lots of baggage. But God was using them to accomplish His will. And He was fighting their battles for them.

God wants to fight your battles for you today. Whatever you're facing, He knows and He cares. He is just as strong and powerful today as He was in Moses' and Joshua's day. Ask Him for help. The tale of your life will turn out so much better if you do.

Lord God, You chose to be my warrior.
Please fight this battle for me today: [name battle]. Amen.

Chosen for the Miraculous

*Now therefore stand still and see this great thing
that the L*ORD *will do before your eyes.*

1 SAMUEL 12:16 ESV

Not only is Christ our champion, but He is also our miracle worker. At times we need His supernatural intervention in our lives. There are things we cannot do for ourselves, things that lie outside the realm of human possibility. We call these things "miracles."

Miracles probably happen all around us every day, and we just don't recognize them. Think of the miles you travel in your car every day, passing other cars, just a few inches from death if one of you veers into the other lane.

Think of the intricacies of our bodies and the regular pattern of our hearts that continue to beat for a lifetime once they have begun that process in the womb.

Think of the dangers that could happen to our children for which we can't possibly be prepared. There are so many tragedies that could occur in the average household, but they don't.

If you look at it that way, just being alive is a miracle. And when you throw in a few extra things, even ill-advised risks that we take or the dismissal of the need to check up on our health, you understand that miracles happen every day. And yet at times God lets one happen in such a way that we glorify Him for what has taken place.

*Dear Lord, You are a miracle worker, and I thank You for all the
times You kept me and my family safe and we didn't even know
it. Let me recognize Your blessings when I see them. Amen.*

Chosen for a Purpose

We know that to those who love God, who are called according to his plan, everything that happens fits into a pattern for good.
Romans 8:28 Phillips

You, my friend, are chosen for a purpose and all the things in your life are working together in a pattern for good. This doesn't mean that every single event in your life *is* good, but that it is in the pattern! As a recipe uses a variety of ingredients and a puzzle uses some odd-looking pieces and a painting uses ugly background strokes, so our lives are a mixture of good and bad, but our Lord redeems them and puts them together in ways that will amaze us someday.

If we look into the record of the Bible, we can see that this is certainly true. Many of those great faith heroes endured very unpleasant pieces in the pattern—Joseph, Job, Ruth, Mary, Paul. But the stories of their lives are beautiful because of the purpose to which God made everything conform. He will do the same for you.

Father, thank You for making me for a purpose. Today I know the events in my life are part of that pattern. Help me to stay faithful. In Jesus' name, amen.

Chosen for Preparation

"I will go before you and make the crooked places straight."
ISAIAH 45:2 NKJV

As a little girl, I loved riding my bike. I rode on sidewalks and driveways and green grass. Sometimes our whole family would go on bike rides around town, with my parents carting my youngest brother on a seat on one of their bikes. Of course, as any kid knows, the flat spaces are best for bike riding. The downhill places are good. But steep climbs are challenging—you may have to stand on the pedals and exert more energy to keep going.

I wonder if that's how the ancient Israelites felt about the ways in which God was leading them. True, some of it was their own fault. Their rebellion would land them in adversity or captivity, and they would cry out to God. But often they couldn't see that the difficult spots were giving them faith muscle.

On the other hand, God promised them that He would straighten out the crooked places, the places where Satan was trying to defeat His plan. I believe God promises us the same today. We will have to endure the mountains, the valleys, and the challenging roads, but He will go before us and handle the traps of the enemy. Satan has planned to destroy us, but he is no match for our God.

*God, today I ask You to prepare my day. Give me strength
for the challenges, and protect me from the snares that
Satan has laid for me. I trust in You today. Amen.*

Chosen for Obtaining

And so, after he had patiently endured,
he obtained the promise.
HEBREWS 6:15 NKJV

Advertising is focused on obtaining. Whether it's shiny hair or an organized closet or whiter teeth, every commercial is calculated to get us to want to obtain something. When you realize this, you gain a little bit of power over the subliminal, but the lure of what is promised is still substantial.

I think Abraham felt that way. The lure of having an heir, his own flesh and blood, was so strong that he almost got sidetracked. When the enemy tried to get him to give up on the child of promise through Sarah's suggestion about Hagar, he listened. He wondered if this might be his only chance to be a father. He went along with the detour. But in the end, God brought him back by allowing the conflict between Sarah and Hagar to show what was really going on.

When the angels showed up at Abraham's camp to tell him that soon he would have a son, Sarah laughed. Perhaps she had bought Satan's "commercials" about their future.

But God kept His word: Sarah conceived in her old age, and Isaac was born. And today the Jewish people are a great nation, more than can be numbered by any of us, more than the stars of the sky and the sand of the seashore.

Abraham was chosen for obtaining the promise God made. And so are you. Wait patiently for it.

Father God, You are El Shaddai: God Almighty.
Today, like Abraham, I choose to wait for
Your promises to come true. Amen.

Chosen for Declaration

May He grant you according to your heart's desire and
fulfill all your purpose. We will rejoice in your salvation,
and in the name of our God we will set up our
banners! May the Lᴏʀᴅ fulfill all your petitions.

Pꜱᴀʟᴍ 20:4–5 ɴᴋᴊᴠ

In ancient times, kings had banners or standards under which their troops marched or rode. This was a way to identify the armies as well as a way to celebrate victory. Flags also were carried in both the Revolutionary War and the Civil War. The standard bearer held a position of both honor and risk. He was the point of encouragement for the soldiers and would help them distinguish where they were if they became separated in battle, as in the cry "Rally 'round the flag!" But he was also a natural target for sharpshooters because of this very thing.

In Psalm 20 David declares that he will set up banners in the name of God as a signal to all that he was resting in the salvation, the rescue, of the Almighty. Like David, we can demonstrate faith that God is in charge of the battle and will fulfill the purpose He has for us.

Today you may feel weary in battle. You may have been wounded. You may not know where your comrades are. You may be wondering about the purpose of your commander. Take heart! Lift up the banner of your King! Rally around the flag of His faithfulness!

O Lord, I declare that You are Jehovah Nissi: The Lord Is
My Banner. Today I will lift high the banner of
Your greatness and trust in You. Amen.

Chosen for Future Joy

"Blessed is she who believed, for there will be a fulfillment of those things which were told her from the Lord."
LUKE 1:45 NKJV

Delayed gratification is one of life's disciplines. It is tempting to want to have the happiness now, whether it be from a new phone or new car, a longed-for vacation, or a wardrobe change. We want it now. We want to feel the joy of using something better.

But life is a process that involves the passing of time, more like a fine restaurant where the chef specially prepares each dish than a drive-through where meals are assembly-line ready. Admittedly, there are more important things than a phone or vacation. In our spiritual lives, we may be waiting for the opening of a ministry opportunity or an answer to prayer in the life of one of our family members. We may not see any way in the present that it will happen.

But take courage from the story of Mary. Elizabeth's words to her in this verse remind us that Mary had to endure some very difficult days in her pregnancy as she waited for vindication in the eyes of her family and Joseph and even her hometown. And maybe there were times when it all seemed like a dream to her. But the baby that was born months later proved to her beyond any doubt that God's words were true. And the joy of that must have been worth the angst before.

You are chosen for future joy. Keep hanging on.

Lord, today I know I need to wait for Your fulfillment. Help me to be content in the promise of future joy. Amen.

Chosen for Completion

*Being confident of this very thing, that He who has begun a good
work in you will complete it until the day of Jesus Christ.*
PHILIPPIANS 1:6 NKJV

Gomer was married to a prophet, but she was not happy. She didn't
want the life she had, so she left him and her children to pursue a life
with another man. But Hosea, her husband, wouldn't give up on her. He
came after her and found her in a pitiful condition. He took her home
and cared for her and gave her back his love as her husband.

Gomer's name means "completion." And she was a symbol of the
nation of Israel as the wandering beloved on whom God would not give
up. He promised to complete the work of saving the world through
the line of Christ, and He will do it. He finishes what He starts.

In your life, there may be some things that feel unfinished. In fact,
you may have sinned and left your first love. Satan wants to tell you
that you are a lost cause and the future is wrecked. But God tells you
to return to Him and watch as He completes His good work in you.

Perhaps you are not a rebel but are just confused about how God is
leading you. You too can be confident that He is at work and will finish
what He began in you in His time.

*Heavenly Father, thank You for starting Your good work
in me. I trust You to bring me to completion. Amen.*

Chosen for Covenant

*Therefore know that the Lord your God, He is God, the faithful
God who keeps covenant and mercy for a thousand generations
with those who love Him and keep His commandments.*
DEUTERONOMY 7:9 NKJV

It is one thing to *make* a covenant. It is quite another to *keep* a covenant.

Perhaps the most important covenant many of us will enter into is that of marriage. In the past, marriage has been called a contract, an arrangement, even a type of legal union. But, in God's eyes, marriage is a lifelong covenant between two dual image-bearers, male and female. It is not primarily for convenience or pleasure or status; it is to show His glory to the world.

Satan has attacked the concept of covenant through his attack on marriage. By getting earthly husbands to abandon their wives, he chips away at the earthly reflection of God who is ever faithful. If he can incite human wives to do their own thing and leave their husbands, he strikes a blow at the image of the Church as the bride of Christ. When human marriages split up, the idea of a lasting covenant is marred.

But we know that Satan cannot truly destroy what God creates. And he can never change the nature of God nor the foundational truths His Word teaches. The Old Testament reminds us that God will always keep His covenant. And He calls us to do the same.

*Faithful God, thank You for keeping Your word for generations.
Show me today how I can reflect You in the earthly
covenants I have made. Amen.*

Chosen for Establishment

Commit your works to the LORD,
and your thoughts will be established.

PROVERBS 16:3 NKJV

When I think of something being established, I think about concrete.

If you've ever been around a building site or perhaps have built your own home, you know that concrete is used in the foundation and sometimes in the driveway and other places where a firm foundation is needed. Before the actual cement can be delivered and poured, the contractor builds forms to hold it. These wooden structures contain the wet substance and give it a shape in which to dry.

After all is prepared, the cement arrives and is poured from the truck while workers with long squeegees push it into place and smooth it out. Then they let it dry and cure. Within a few days, the foundation of that house is established. It will take some serious storm damage to move it!

You and I are told that God wants to establish us as His daughters. He wants to make us beautiful temples of His grace. But we must be on a solid footing in order for Him to do that. So He calls us to commit our works to Him—all we hope and dream, all we do, all we plan to be and do in the future.

What are you doing today? How can you commit to the Lord the relationships and activities of your day?

Heavenly Father, Your Word says that You want to establish
me. Today I bring You this: [name what you want to
commit to the Lord]. I commit it to You. Amen.

Chosen to See Goodness

*I would have lost heart, unless I had believed that I would
see the goodness of the Lᴏʀᴅ in the land of the living.*
Pѕᴀʟᴍ 27:13 ɴᴋᴊᴠ

Our eyes long to see good things. I believe that's why many of us really like the fall of the year. It is a visual feast. Brilliantly colored leaves, bulging, multicolored pumpkins and gourds, cornstalks and scarecrows, azure blue skies, plaid scarves, and all the rest.

God chose to give us seasons for a variety of reasons. When we see the fragile entrance of spring and the warm rush of summer or the quiet chill of winter in the world around us, we are reminded of His goodness. He is the keeper of the seasons. He is the One who gives us all these things to enjoy. He is reminding us that we can trust Him. If He can keep the world going and even maintain the cycle of seasons for thousands of years, He can work in the little details of our lives.

The psalmist says that it is easy to lose heart unless we believe in the goodness of the Lord. To stay on track, we must read His Word and believe in His name and focus our eyes on the proof we see around us. He will bring about what He has promised. He calls us to believe that in every seasonal change.

*Lord God, You have made the earth and the seasons. You are good,
and all Your promises will come to pass. I trust You. Amen.*

Chosen for Help

He shall call upon Me, and I will answer him;
I will be with him in trouble.
PSALM 91:15 NKJV

If you are a mom, you know about those calls for help. They can come at any time and in any place—middle of the night, from the bedroom or bathroom, in a store, at a friend's house. They are a distress signal. And, of course, a mother responds immediately.

Experts say that if moms go to their babies when they cry, the infants will learn that they are being cared for and will be more secure. Of course, grandmothers remind us that forever picking up crying babies will ensure that we will never have a moment's peace because the babies will become spoiled. Somewhere between the two pieces of advice lies wisdom and balance. But we do know that children who are neglected and abused learn to stop crying out for help.

We don't ever have to worry about that in the case of our Father God. He has promised that He will answer when we call. He knows that sometimes we cry out after we have gotten ourselves in a mess, but He comes to us anyway with both comfort and discipline. He doesn't tell us only to call on Him during certain hours or in certain settings. Like a human mother, His ears are open to our cries (Psalm 34:15). He will answer us in our trouble.

Dear Lord, let me never forget that You are my help
and the source of my strength. Thank You that
I can call on You in my trouble. Amen.

Chosen for a Future

For I know the thoughts that I think toward you,
says the Lord, thoughts of peace and not of
evil, to give you a future and a hope.
JEREMIAH 29:11 NKJV

Probably nothing is more encouraging to us than to know that God is thinking of our future.

As little girls, we dream about our futures. We imagine meeting a handsome, loving man and getting married, having babies, and keeping house. Sometimes we imagine ourselves to be doctors or nurses, veterinarians or teachers, chefs or cosmetologists, lawyers or scientists.

As we become teens, our dreams and plans begin to take shape—to study in college or to start a vocation after high school. We are continually aware of the young men around us, watching for that perfect one who might be Mr. Right.

In adult life, we may look back on our childhood and adolescence and see the differences between our plans and the actual lives we are living. Some of the differences may be due to alterations in our dreams over which we had no control. We might think that the future has come and gone and there is nothing for which we can hope lying ahead of us.

But that is untrue. The future in Christ always lies ahead of us. And the best is yet to come. Satan will do his best to defeat us with the reroutes of our earthly lives so far, but he is no match for the One who plans our futures. Remember that today.

Dear Lord, I had plans for my life, and not all of them were fulfilled,
but I trust my future to You. I know I have hope in You. Amen.

Chosen for Reality

*Do not be deceived, God is not mocked; for whatever a man
sows, that he will also reap. For he who sows to his flesh
will of the flesh reap corruption, but he who sows to
the Spirit will of the Spirit reap everlasting life.*

GALATIANS 6:7–8 NKJV

Humans have the ability to convince ourselves of what we want to believe. The culture tells us, at Satan's prompting, that we can "sow wild oats" and get away with it. But God's Word says that isn't so, and to believe it is to believe an untruth about our Creator.

God is never mocked. He always has the last word, the last say, the final judgment.

Satan wants you to believe that you are insignificant, a result of a random evolutionary process. If that is so, then there is no God and you are not responsible to Him for your actions.

Satan wants you to believe that gender is a matter of personal preference. If that is true, then our design as human women means nothing and has no bearing on God's purpose for us.

Satan wants you to believe that a baby in the womb is merely tissue that a woman can dispose of. If that is true, then abortion is acceptable as a way of removing the unwanted consequences of one's sexual freedom.

But all of these things are false. We have the wonderful opportunity to check in with God's reality today and to "sow to the Spirit." That will reap us everlasting life.

*Lord, help me today to accept Your reality about the world and
to recognize the lies of the enemy. In Jesus' name, amen.*

Chosen for Recollection

This I recall to my mind, therefore I have hope. Through the LORD's mercies we are not consumed, because His compassions fail not. They are new every morning; great is Your faithfulness.

<small>LAMENTATIONS 3:21–23 NKJV</small>

It is good for us to recall things. God made our brains with the wonderful ability to remember. Memory is made because the neural wiring of the brain is actually changed as it records experiences and information. And unless our brains have been damaged in some way, we can bring up those memories and recall the emotions associated with them.

Perhaps you know that the sense of smell is the one most closely associated with memory. Inhaling the scent of a certain place or item can transport us back to an experience or person. Babies can distinguish the smell of their mothers from other women; this God-given instinct is a protective bonding device. And as we grow, memories, whether connected to smell or not, become embedded in our minds.

We should use this ability to help us focus on the strength we have in our Lord. The writer of Lamentations reminds us that we have hope when we call to mind the things God has done for us in the past. His faithfulness over the years, morning after morning, encourages us to believe the truth that He is the same today. There is no better way to use our memories.

Almighty Father, You are the faithful One. I remember how You have helped me in the past, and I look to You as my source today. Amen.

Chosen for Keeping

For He shall give His angels charge over you,
to keep you in all your ways.
PSALM 91:11 NKJV

Angels are popular icons. We find comfort in the idea that some heavenly being is watching over us.

At times this belief in angels gets taken too far, beyond biblical parameters. For instance, although it is a popular notion, there is no teaching in scripture that tells us our deceased loved ones become angels watching out for us. And there is no evidence that we ourselves become angels when we die. God created them angelic and us human; that stays the same.

When I was a little girl, I had a picture on the wall in my bedroom of a brother and sister walking on a bridge across a chasm. Far down below was rushing water. The bridge was rickety with slats missing. And hovering above those children was a beautiful angel, keeping watch, guarding their steps. The memory of that picture still makes me smile today.

I don't know if that picture is correct, and I don't know all the ways in which God uses His angels, but I do know that He sometimes sends them to help us. The God who promises to be with us always is also the Master of the heavenly host, and we are chosen to be kept.

Father in heaven, thank You for creating angels and for
the promise that I am being kept by Your power.
You are my protection. Amen.

Chosen for Blooming

"The LORD will guide you continually, and satisfy your soul in drought, and strengthen your bones; you shall be like a watered garden, and like a spring of water, whose waters do not fail."
ISAIAH 58:11 NKJV

We sometimes experience emotional seasons of drought. Illness, marriage conflict, challenges in parenting, church difficulties, relationship changes, aging, and more can feel like barren places. We wonder if we will make it or if our flourishing days are past.

One of the greatest inventions for farmers in arid areas is the irrigation system. In some geographical locations, rain is scarce and the dry season is long. Instead of relinquishing the idea of growing things, smart people devised ways to get water into the fields. Now, however hot and parched the day, life-giving water can be delivered to thirsty roots.

God wants to do that for us in our difficult seasons. He has an irrigation system for grace that never fails. When the days are long and hard, we can call on Him. His supply is never short, and His power source is always on.

The Bible often refers to godly people as flourishing plants or trees beside water; we are to be lush and green and healthy. But this is not possible on a continuing basis without His supernatural grace. As we stay connected to Him, we can continue to bloom. We were chosen for it.

Lord, my life feels like a drought right now. Send Your life-giving supply of grace into my soul, and help me to bloom. In Jesus' name, amen.

Chosen for Wisdom

See then that you walk circumspectly, not as fools but as wise,
redeeming the time, because the days are evil.
EPHESIANS 5:15–16 NKJV

Circumspectly is not a word we use much. It was borrowed from the Latin *circumspectus,* from *circumspicere,* "to look around, be cautious." We can understand this if we remember that the word *circumference* means the measure of something round.

So, the apostle Paul was admonishing the Ephesian Christians to walk, or to live, in a cautious way, looking around for ways to redeem or make the best use of their time. This is good advice for us too.

Many things compete for our time. Some of them are urgent—caring for a baby, finishing a work project for a deadline, making dinner for hungry children, and so on. These things must be done today, now. Other things are important but not immediate—investing in our marriage, taking care of our health, organizing the basement. An obvious hierarchy of need and priority is involved.

And that is what God wants us to understand. We must spend our time on the things that matter most, especially in light of the things happening in our world. One of our most vital realizations must be that others do not know Christ and we have the privilege to let the light of our lives shine before them. Sometimes we may need to speak to them about Christ. We are chosen for wisdom, and that includes putting focus on the most important things.

Lord Jesus, shine forth from me today, and let me live
circumspectly in the way I use my time. Amen.

Chosen for Settling

May the God of all grace, who called us to His eternal glory
by Christ Jesus, after you have suffered a while, perfect,
establish, strengthen, and settle you.

1 PETER 5:10 NKJV

When I think of settling, I think of the days of the American westward expansion and the people we call "the settlers." These hardy souls packed up what they owned in ox-drawn covered wagons and traveled long weary months to claim a piece of land and make a home and a future. They "settled" in the land and helped to tame it and inhabit it for generations to come.

There are many other applications of the word *settle* of course. But the main idea remains the same—to put down roots, to be attached to a certain place, to be firm in one's location.

This is the prayer that the apostle Peter had for the Christians under his ministry, and it is the plan and promise of God toward us today. He will establish and strengthen and settle us as we stay in relationship with Him and open to His grace. Our part is to obey the Holy Spirit's voice when He speaks to us and to be intentional about spending time with the Lord in His Word and in prayer. As we purposefully invest in our spiritual lives, He does the settling part.

You and I are chosen to be settled in God's grace. Let Him work in you today.

Dear God, I want to be settled for eternity.
I draw near to You today. Amen.

Chosen for Revival

Though I walk in the midst of trouble, You will revive me;
You will stretch out Your hand against the wrath of
my enemies, and Your right hand will save me.
PSALM 138:7 NKJV

The word *revival* often conjures up images of church services where an evangelist preaches a series of meetings. This was very common a few years back in many evangelical denominations. And this is one practical application of the word *revival*.

But, in actuality, the reason those meetings were called revivals is because that was the intent—to revive the Church, God's people. Realizing that drawing near to God results in spiritual renewal, pastors tried to provide these kinds of opportunities for their church members.

But we can experience revival without waiting for a special service. The psalmist acknowledges that God will revive him even in the midst of trouble. He will bring energy and renewed hope to him when the enemy is attacking.

What kind of trouble are you in today? Is there a situation in your life for which you have no energy? Are you spiritually out of breath and anemic? Turn today to the One who revives us, knowing He has promised to do it. You are chosen to be His, and that means He will revive you if you ask.

Holy Spirit, breathe Your life into me and revive my heart
so I can honor You today in every situation. Amen.

Chosen for Thankfulness

Give thanks to the Lord, for he is good, for his steadfast love endures
forever. Give thanks to the God of gods, for his steadfast love
endures forever. Give thanks to the Lord of lords,
for his steadfast love endures forever.
PSALM 136:1–3 ESV

Thankfulness is an action that even unbelievers embrace today. Research shows that having a grateful attitude promotes health. The puzzling thing is, however, that those who do not believe in God have no center on which to focus their gratefulness. There is no one to receive the thanks offered up. Perhaps psychologists believe there is benefit in just having a warm feeling inside about one's blessings. But how very much is missed if one does not know the source of every good gift!

We expect to see admonitions to thankfulness around Thanksgiving. But as Christ followers, we recognize that God is good all year long. As David says, God's love endures forever. We should give thanks for this. If He has done good for us today, He will do good for us tomorrow. His very nature is good, and that is why we can rest in the promise that He is working out a plan in us.

Those who don't know Christ can still be thankful, but they do not have the assurance of His promises like those who believe. You are chosen to be thankful. Get started right now!

Thank You, O Lord, for Your steadfast love
and for Your promises to me. Amen.

Chosen for an Unchanging Christ

Jesus Christ is the same yesterday and today and forever.
HEBREWS 13:8 ESV

Marriage is a commitment to a person who might change. That is one of the most terrifying aspects of preparing for marriage. As well as you know the person you are about to marry, the truth is that people do change over time. That doesn't mean it will be life-altering changes, but at times that happens. Sometimes a spouse walks away from following Christ or experiences an emotional breakdown or changes his or her philosophy on parenting or ministry or other responsibilities. This will bring challenges into the marriage and call for adjustment. At other times the changes are small. And all of us change over the course of years, even if only in preferences that really make no difference in the big picture of life.

But the possibility of a person's decision to change is one aspect of marriage that cannot be controlled. So both husband and wife must proceed on their wedding day, determined to remain committed and trusting God to keep the other person on the same track.

In our relationship with Jesus, we never have to worry about this. He doesn't change His future plans, His purpose for us, His love, His compassion, His truth, His character, or His nature. He is always the same. We can depend on Him being always constant, always faithful. Perhaps someone in your life has changed recently and you feel blown about and confused. Remember today's promise and depend on the changeless One to help you.

You are unchanging, O Lord, and I praise You.
Give me strength for my adjustments today. Amen.

Surrounded and Glorified

*"I will be to her a wall of fire all around,
declares the LORD, and I will be the glory in her midst."*
ZECHARIAH 2:5 ESV

*I have likened the daughter of Zion
to a comely and delicate woman.*
JEREMIAH 6:2 KJV

The Lord says that the new Jerusalem will be as beautiful as a bride prepared for her groom on her wedding day. "And I saw the holy city, new Jerusalem, coming down out of heaven from God, prepared as a bride adorned for her husband" (Revelation 21:2 ESV).

So in this promise from the book of Jeremiah, God is speaking directly about His divine protection of the city that is at the heart of the plan of redemption. Jesus was crucified just outside this city. Into the gates of this city the reigning Messiah will enter someday. It is a sacred place, a protected place. We must never forget that truth as we observe prophecies being fulfilled around it.

But as Christian women, we might take this promise as a comfort to us as well. Many times we feel unprotected and vulnerable. We have overwhelming life responsibilities that bring insecurities and fears.

God has promised to be with us. In the words of this promise, He will be a wall of fire around us and a glory inside us. That sounds like ultimate protection to me.

*Lord, I am Yours, and I need You to surround me
and protect me today. In Jesus' name I pray. Amen.*

The Will and Power

*For it is God who is at work within you, giving you
the will and the power to achieve his purpose.*
PHILIPPIANS 2:13 PHILLIPS

Most of us love a pajama day once in a while. You know, one of those days where you can get up slowly and take your time with breakfast or brunch and not have to hurry anywhere. You can stay in your pajamas and spend downtime without worrying about someone expecting you to be somewhere or to look glamorous. These kinds of days are best when your husband is out of town and the kids are at school and no one needs you for anything. It wouldn't be healthy for us to have these days all the time. But occasionally a pajama day can be a good thing. They're days when you don't have the will nor the energy to do anything.

In the Christian life, there are no pajama days unless you don't care about regressing in your walk with Christ. Every day of our lives we need to be purposeful about living in obedience to God's Word and staying in communication with Him. If we grow careless about our spiritual self-care, we will reap the consequences, and Satan may have an inroad by which to tempt us.

The thing to remember is that God supplies both the will and the willpower to live intentionally for Him. We need to cooperate with that.

*Lord, let me live every day with purpose, depending on You
for the will and the willpower. In Jesus' name, amen.*

Fighting the Enemies

"The LORD your God is he who goes with you to fight for you against your enemies, to give you the victory."

<small>DEUTERONOMY 20:4 ESV</small>

Bullying receives a lot of attention in our schools. It is a problem that needs to be addressed. The world has always had bullies, and many of us remember them from our elementary school days. "Lording it" over those whom one presumes to be weak and defenseless is a perennial flaw of humankind. Though in reality most bullies are more bluff than brawn, they like to present the image that they are fearless and undefeatable. This gives their egos a little more life on which to live. They are like vampires, existing on the blood of others.

God promised His people that He would fight for them against the enemies, the bullies, they would face. He knew that Satan, the ultimate bully, would do his best to scare God's people from making progress in Canaan. He knew that Satan, through these pagan nations, would bluff and bluster and arouse fear of failure in the hearts of the Israelites. But He promised to come to their defense and give them victory.

In a similar way, God will fight for us today. We face the same foe, the cosmic bully, Satan. He wants to stop our spiritual advancement and defeat us. But he is no match for our God. The God of Israel is on our side. He will win the battle if we call on Him.

Almighty God, You are Yahweh Tsebaoth: The Lord of Hosts. You command the armies of heaven. You are the ultimate warrior. I depend on You today to defend me and give me victory. Amen.

These Things Will Come

"Set your heart on the kingdom and his goodness, and all these things will come to you as a matter of course."
MATTHEW 6:33 PHILLIPS

Jesus understood the process of living in this material world, this earth. And furthermore, He, as Creator, wanted human beings to enjoy the provisions, the blessings of this life. God is not a stingy Scrooge, scheming how to hoard blessings in heaven and doling out pitiful scraps to His children. No, the Bible says that He gives us richly all things to enjoy (1 Timothy 6:17). But He wants us to understand that He can provide what we need if we focus our lives on Him rather than on stuff.

There is certainly no sin in having nice things as long as one is being a good manager of the other aspects of his or her life. But to have our focus on the stock market every day or the latest gadget or fashion magazine might not be the best for our spiritual lives.

When Jesus spoke these words, He was surrounded by simple, poor people. For many of them, even obtaining daily food was a struggle. So when He said not to worry about what to eat or what to wear, those were vital issues for them. But the God who feeds the sparrows will feed us. And He knows about the new gadgets too.

Lord, You provide for me the things I need.
I trust You for my wants. Amen.

Wonder and Astonishment

"Look among the nations, and see; wonder and be astounded. For I am doing a work in your days that you would not believe if told."

ㅤHABAKKUK 1:5 ESV

You have to see it to believe it!

Has someone ever said that to you?

Usually it's because the thing is so incredible that only actual vision will confirm it is true. And still sometimes, our eyes deceive us. We visited a museum when our children were young called Ripley's Believe It or Not. Some of the displays were amazing, even unbelievable. Of course, there are some pretty wild aberrations in nature and in people (like two-headed calves and unusually tall people), so some of the reports were actually true. But others, it seemed, might have been relying on a bit of trickery, the result of optical illusion.

Our eyes, though magnificent, can be deceived. It is another of the fascinating ways God made us. Many magicians employ this in what they call "sleight of hand." The human hand is actually faster than the human eye.

But God told the nation of Israel that He was really doing an astounding work. This was supernatural power on display. He doesn't have to pretend or use sleight of hand. He is the Master of the Universe, and He has all the power.

Perhaps you need to hear this today because something is wrong in your life. You need a supernatural answer. The prophet Habakkuk says you've come to the right One!

I praise You, O God, because You do mighty works.
I lay my problem out before You today. Amen.

Taught by Him

Thus says the LORD, your Redeemer, the Holy One of Israel:
"I am the LORD your God, who teaches you to profit,
who leads you in the way you should go."
ISAIAH 48:17 ESV

Teachers are important people. They train our minds. They instill in us things we remember even into adulthood. They are voices for truth.

You probably had a favorite teacher or two when you were in elementary school. I remember my second-grade teacher, Miss Hatcher. She had red hair and was very strict. Coming from a homeschool environment, I struggled to acclimate to the new routines and rules and curriculum. I went through a stage of intense fear of her. But by the end of that year, I had grown to love her. She helped me learn phonics and improve my reading. And she showed me that having rules can keep everyone going in the right direction.

God is our teacher. He said to Israel, through the prophet Isaiah, that He would teach them what they needed to profit. He wasn't referring to mere financial profit but to spiritual gains, to advancing in relationship with Him. He leads us in the way we should go.

We should reverence God but not hide from Him. We should understand that His rules are to keep us on the right track. We will come to love Him more if we stay in the school and submit to His instruction.

Thank You, Lord, for being my Instructor.
Help me learn what I need to know today. Amen.

Just and Upright

*"For I will proclaim the name of the Lord; ascribe greatness
to our God! The Rock, his work is perfect, for all his
ways are justice. A God of faithfulness and
without iniquity, just and upright is he."*
DEUTERONOMY 32:3–4 ESV

Judges are necessary in this life. When there is a dispute about the law, a judge can make the decision. When a crime has been committed, the judge can issue the appropriate sentence. God instituted earthly authority for our good. It is not His will that we be undisciplined people left to our own devices. He wants for our authority structure in government to help us.

When a judge is nominated to the bench, he or she must go through a vetting process. Personal background is examined, and any breach of conduct or character is brought to the front. The idea is to make sure that this person has a character and track record worthy of the job.

The character and track record of the Lord is impeccable. He is a God of faithfulness and without iniquity. And that is why we can trust Him.

At times in our lives, we are tempted to doubt His wisdom and His Word. Satan makes sure to bring up all the little doubts or show us someone else who claims to be a Christ follower but manages his or her life differently from the way we do ours.

In any of these situations, we turn our attention back to where it belongs—to the bench, to the Judge. There we are safe.

*Lord God, I focus my gaze on Your righteousness today.
Thank You for being a just Judge. Amen.*

Delight and Desires

*Delight yourself in the L*ORD*,*
and he will give you the desires of your heart.
PSALM 37:4 ESV

Maybe you delight in a new book to read, a fragrant cup of coffee, an afternoon with a friend, the discovery of a new shop, cuddling a newborn baby, or looking through your wedding pictures. Whatever it is, the feeling of delight is usually related to some desire being fulfilled.

God tells us to delight ourselves in Him even before the blessings arrive. He knows that we need to guide our hearts in the ways they should go. And when we do that, He will fulfill our desires because we have our priorities right. If He indulged our wants and preferences from the very beginning, He would raise spoiled, bratty children. But instead, He calls us to focus on Him and then promises to fill our lives with blessings.

This verse can be used by those who preach that God will give you everything you want. If you desire it, they say, God must have put the desire there, and He intends to fulfill it. The Bible does not affirm this idea, but it does say that we will have all we need in this moment to bring Him glory—that may be a lot or it may be hardly anything. The apostle Paul said that he had learned to be content with any number of blessings (Philippians 4:11). That should be our goal too.

Lord, thank You for the blessings You give me.
Today I hold them with surrendered hands and ask
You to help me learn true delight in who You are. Amen.

Far Stronger

You, my children, who belong to God have already defeated
this spirit, because the one who lives in you is far
stronger than the anti-Christ in the world.

1 John 4:4 Phillips

My brothers used to like the adventures of superheroes. Those larger-than-life characters could take on any enemy, any force, and triumph. Human beings are drawn to victory, to those who are stronger, wiser, smarter, bigger, faster. Perhaps this is the reason for the popularity of comic books and television shows about characters like the Lone Ranger and Superman. These stalwart defenders of freedom and righteousness could not be overcome by anything the scriptwriters threw at them. They always found a way around the villain, were always stronger than the speeding train, could always ride harder and shoot faster than their opponents. They made us believe that we could be strong and victorious too.

God made us with a fascination with strength and triumph. And He reminds us that He is the ultimate force in this world. He is the One we can trust to defeat every foe that rises against us. He is the One who can empower us to experience victory over the antichrist spirit at work in our world. He has already defeated Satan at the cross, and He will win the future, final victory.

God, You are far stronger than he who is in the world, the
antichrist spirit. I look to You today for victory in my life. Amen.

Hiding Places

You are my hiding place; You shall preserve me from trouble;
You shall surround me with songs of deliverance. Selah.
PSALM 32:7–8 NKJV

Hide-and-seek is a favorite pastime of children everywhere. The adrenalin is pumping, and screams here and there tell us some are being found. But, oh, the exhilaration of being the last one still hiding. To have chosen a refuge that was not discovered is a triumph.

More than a children's game is our experience as believers. Satan is on the prowl, like a roaring lion, the apostle Peter says (1 Peter 5:8). He is looking for us, trying to ferret us out, wanting to devour us.

But the psalmist reminds us that God is our hiding place. He surrounds us with songs of deliverance. Those songs have power to keep Satan at bay. These notes of rejoicing in the almighty power of God are like a shield all around us. We are surrounded by His praises as with an army.

God does not let us evade spiritual battles, but there are times when He protects us from a particular attack of Satan. However He chooses to work, we know that His power is infinite.

Playing hide-and-seek in the dark adds to the excitement, and often it seems especially dark when Satan is tracking us. But the Lord Jehovah will be our refuge. No one can get to us when we are in His care. He is truly "base."

Lord, today I hide in You from the attack of the enemy.
You are my hiding place. Amen.

Ordained in the Womb

*"Before I formed you in the womb I knew
you; before you were born I sanctified you;
I ordained you a prophet to the nations."*
JEREMIAH 1:5 NKJV

We know a lot more about life in the womb than they did in Bible days. The development of sonography and other imaging devices have allowed us to see into that private, sacred place and behold the amazing development of new life.

That same technology has bequeathed us the horrible tools with which to sever these children from the womb and discard them. Abortion takes from us millions of lives that were ordained for a special purpose.

In Jeremiah 1:5 the Lord told Jeremiah that he was known and that he was set apart (or sanctified) for a specific work. He was ordained for a special purpose in life. We have no reason to believe that God does not have a specific purpose for every single human who is conceived. If a life is prevented from blooming into full maturity, perhaps God will give that person the opportunity to use his or her gifts in the heavenly kingdom.

Today you need to know that you were in God's heart even before your mother conceived you. God knew about your future existence and planned a place for you. How He keeps track of all the babies and miscarriages and abortions and infant deaths is beyond understanding. But He is God, after all. If we could understand it, we would be divine too.

You are not an afterthought, mistake, or accident. You were ordained to be here. Chosen for a purpose.

Creator God, thank You for Your plan in my life. Help us to value the unborn, these precious people already known to You. Amen.

A Shield for You

Every word of God is pure; He is a shield
to those who put their trust in Him.
PROVERBS 30:5 NKJV

If you have read any of the Chronicles of Narnia by C. S. Lewis, you remember that there are epic battles involved and that the kings and queens of Narnia wear incredible battle dress, complete with swords and shields and other necessary items. They can fight like champions, and they do.

I remember my brother creating elaborate costumes when we were children at play. To enhance whatever story line we were currently illustrating, he would craft the accoutrements of a cowboy or an astronaut or a soldier. I remember him making a shield for swordplay. It couldn't have been very sturdy, but it was usable for his purposes and it protected him from many an enemy arrow, I'm sure.

You and I need a shield. We are on a battlefield of faith. The enemy is shooting fiery darts at us (Ephesians 6:16). We need Someone we can depend on.

Our God does not want us to be left unprotected in our war with Satan. Like the children in Narnia, we can do nothing on our own. Only the mighty Lion of the tribe of Judah can change the course of events. And while we wait for His will, we trust in Him to shield us.

Mighty Father, today I face my enemy, Satan, who wants to
defeat me. Please be my shield. In Jesus' name, amen.

The Mighty Word

*So shall My word be that goes forth from My mouth; it shall not
return to Me void, but it shall accomplish what I please,
and it shall prosper in the thing for which I sent it.*

ISAIAH 55:11 NKJV

Most of us have owned a Bible all our lives. We are familiar with its stories and its teachings, and it is easy to forget how powerful it actually is because we are so used to it.

As Christ followers, you and I have been chosen to share the Good News with others. We have a responsibility not only to be visible witnesses through our lives and interactions with others but also to be vocal witnesses through our conversations and encouragement. God has no voice on earth except ours.

Sharing the Gospel can be discouraging at times. Many of the people we befriend in culture are so far removed from the actual truth of the Gospel that it takes awhile for us even to lay a foundation on which to begin to explain. The enemy uses bits and pieces that people hear from grandmothers and television preachers and then mixes it with a good bit of opinion and tradition and makes them believe things about God and heaven that aren't true. The only way to combat this is with the truth. And God promises that when we speak His Word, it will have an effect. God's Word is never shared in vain.

*Lord, use my lips today to speak Your truth.
Thank You for choosing me to be Your mouthpiece. Amen.*

Nothing Too Hard

*"Behold, I am the L*ORD*, the God of all flesh.*
Is anything too hard for me?"
JEREMIAH 32:27 ESV

At times, God chooses to limit His power according to His purposes.

For example, when Jesus came to earth, into the womb of a human mother, He voluntarily limited His own power and knowledge so that He could become like us. He was a baby in every human sense of the word, except that He had no sin nature. He was not an infant with perfect knowledge, realizing that He was a baby. No, He was a real baby.

There are other instances in the biblical record or in our lives when God chooses to limit His own power. This does not mean that He cannot change the situation, but because of a higher purpose, He chooses not to allow Himself to change it. This is not a conflict in His nature, but rather a singleness of purpose for our good and His glory.

Today God may have chosen to limit His power in your life. He may have chosen You for a higher purpose. Rest in His care and knowledge.

Heavenly Father, You can do anything. And I trust
You when You choose not to intervene. Amen.

Grace and Glory

*For the L<small>ORD</small> God is a sun and shield; the L<small>ORD</small> will
give grace and glory; no good thing will He
withhold from those who walk uprightly.*

P<small>SALM</small> 84:11 <small>NKJV</small>

The words *grace* and *glory* go together like the perfect pairing of cosmetics. One enhances the other.

Women have their favorite lotions and potions, as a friend of mine likes to say. Whatever brand you use, Oil of Olay or Mary Kay or something else, you have a daily beauty regimen that you use to combat the effects of gravity and aging. As we get older, we begin to slather on the good stuff, trying to keep some of our youthful glow. It is a losing battle, eventually, but being good stewards of our femininity in biblical ways is certainly appropriate.

The Bible, though, does speak of inner beauty as being the most important. A relationship with the Creator of the universe will actually enhance both our inner and outer looks. And He gifts us with grace and glory.

Every woman needs grace—in her own life and to give out to others. She also needs glory—God's majesty radiating out from her to others. Just as we put on our lotions, we are responsible to put on grace and glory. And we do that by spending time in His presence. When we have that piece of life right, the other pieces more quickly fall into proper place.

You are chosen for grace and glory today. Put them on.

*Lord Jesus, radiate Your beauty through me today.
Be the grace and glory in me. Amen.*

Boasting and Magnifying

*I will bless the L**ORD** at all times; His praise shall continually
be in my mouth. My soul shall make its boast in the L**ORD**;
the humble shall hear of it and be glad. Oh, magnify
the L**ORD** with me, and let us exalt His name together.*

PSALM 34:1–3 NKJV

Think of a person who you don't like to be around. Often the person has too high an opinion of himself or herself and continually talks about things he or she has done. No one likes a braggart. We believe that you shouldn't "toot your own horn," as the saying goes. It is unappealing and unattractive.

The psalmist says that he will boast in the Lord. Blessing the Lord God at all times, being glad in His presence, and exalting His name—these actions tell others the Good News and bring them into knowledge of our God.

You are chosen to be a vessel of honor for the Lord. He wants to shine Himself through you today. Like a magnifying glass, you can bring His glory into better focus for those around you because they can see it illustrated in your life.

Today, choose to magnify the One who chose you.

*Father in heaven, I will not boast of myself, but I will do my
best to make You look good to everyone I meet. Amen.*

Taking Captives

For the weapons of our warfare are not carnal but mighty in God for pulling down strongholds, casting down arguments and every high thing that exalts itself against the knowledge of God, bringing every thought into captivity to the obedience of Christ.

2 Corinthians 10:4–5 nkjv

I am a bit of a history buff and especially enjoy learning about the period of World War II. From brief study into this time period, I know that many prisoners of war were taken by both the Axis powers and the Allies. POWs are generally not treated nicely, although officers may be treated slightly better than the enlisted.

God tells us to take captives. We are supposed to manhandle our tempting thoughts. We are not to make them comfortable or give them room to hang around. We are to treat them with military discipline and send them away.

Often, in wartime, POWs would attempt to escape. It was then the job of the other side to thwart their plan and recapture them.

Our thoughts will try to do the same. The devil will be sure at some time to recycle the same temptations and evil thoughts. We must do with them as we did the first time. The Bible tells us that if God is for us, no one can be against us. Don't even consider letting those POWs loose.

Lord, I want to be strong in You and refuse to let any inappropriate thought stay in my mind. Please show me how to be victorious. In Jesus' name, amen.

Unwithering Words

The grass withers, the flower fades,
but the word of our God will stand forever.
ISAIAH 40:8 ESV

I like books, and I have a lot of them. Favorite books are like old friends. Seeing them on my bookshelves gives me a warm, comforting feeling. I love the stories inside the novels, the admonitions inside the devotionals, and the instruction inside the books on marriage or homemaking or ministry. But the words in those books are not divinely inspired. They are helpful but not eternal.

The words in God's Book, however, are everlasting. Scripture tells us they are inspired, or "breathed out by God" (2 Timothy 3:16 ESV). Second Peter 1:21 (ESV) says, "For no prophecy was ever produced by the will of man, but men spoke from God as they were carried along by the Holy Spirit."

This divine book is God's gift to us, the written record of all His promises to us and the story of our redemption. The words will never wither, and their glory will never fade. That promise itself tells us that we can stand on the Bible and know that everything it says is true. The character of the Author of the Bible is eternal, and that means that everything that springs from Him is eternal too.

We can place our firm trust in these wonderful words. They were chosen just for us.

Father God, thank You for Your unfailing,
everlasting words. I will guide my life by them. Amen.

Wings and Muscles

Even youths shall faint and be weary, and young men shall fall exhausted; but they who wait for the LORD shall renew their strength; they shall mount up with wings like eagles; they shall run and not be weary; they shall walk and not faint.
ISAIAH 40:30–31 ESV

I have never been a runner. At times in my life, I have considered it. It seemed like a great way to condition the body and stay fit. But the fact that runners usually run in the morning always discouraged me. And as I have grown older, the wear and tear caused by the constant jolting on the pavement has convinced me that maybe I should leave it to younger people.

I do know that runners need to build up their energy and endurance. I have heard stories of runners who say they started very slowly to build up their stamina and, in the beginning, were not able to last very long. Good nutrition and consistency are, I'm sure, very important.

Most of us have, at some time, observed an eagle in the sky. These majestic birds have strong wings that can stretch out to catch the wind. They are then lifted up in the current to soar.

Both these images are used by the prophet to tell us how God wants to strengthen us in our walk with the Lord. They are analogies that we can understand. We are chosen for strength and stamina, for soaring.

Father in heaven, give me Your supernatural strength today so that I can run and soar. In Jesus' name, amen.

Star Keeper

He determines the number of the stars;
he gives to all of them their names.
PSALM 147:4 ESV

I remember once hearing a radio commercial for a company that would name a star after your loved one in exchange for a certain amount of money. They would send a special certificate noting where the star was located and indicating its new name. They recommended it as the perfect gift for a special occasion, the thing to get someone "who has everything." Indeed, their own star.

All I could think of was this scripture that says God has already named the stars. I wondered if the people who owned that company had read the Bible. Surely, they couldn't have believed it if they thought they could rename them. I wonder if God smiled to Himself at the humans who believed they were the first ones to name a certain star.

The Bible tells us that God created the stars on the fourth day of creation (Genesis 1:16). They have been shining ever since, reminding us whenever we see their luminescent glow in the night sky that if their Designer can count them and name them, He can surely care for us.

You and I can rest in the One who is the star keeper. He has chosen to create us and redeem us and give us eternal life through His Son. We are blessed.

Creator God, Your power amazes me. Since You know and
have named all the stars, I know that You care for me
too and that I can trust You with my life. Amen.

Promise Keeper

"God is not man, that he should lie, or a son of man, that he should change his mind. Has he said, and will he not do it? Or has he spoken, and will he not fulfill it?"
NUMBERS 23:19 ESV

Perhaps one of the most important things to a woman is that a man keep his word to her. Betrayal strikes at the heart with bitter weight. Some of us have experienced the devastation of broken dreams in relationships, even in marriage. It makes one leery of the next experience, uneasy and uncertain. A woman who has experienced betrayal will not be as quick to trust.

Often in scripture God compares His relationship with humanity to a marriage between a husband and wife. He uses marriage language to help us understand His commitment and care and also to help us develop better interaction with our earthly spouses. But the important thing to remember is that He is the perfect type of husband. He truly does love unconditionally. He really does always value us. He doesn't ever abandon us. And He always keeps His word.

Numbers 23:19 is part of a story in the Old Testament where there was conflict between Balaam and Balak over what God wanted Balaam to do. But regardless of man's opinion, the truth of Balaam's words remains. God is not like fallible man. He does not bail out on His promises.

Dear Lord, today help me to remember that I have been chosen as Your beloved and that You always keep Your word. Amen.

Night Vision

*For the eyes of the L*ORD* run to and fro throughout the*
whole earth, to shew himself strong in the behalf
of them whose heart is perfect toward him.
2 CHRONICLES 16:9 KJV

Long before the modern-day military began using night vision technology, the Lord God of heaven could see everything going on with
perfect vision, even at night. At times, when I have been in a city at
night, I imagine the Lord looking down and seeing past all the cables
and rooftops and into the homes and hotels and hovels clustered
together. I think of the trauma and abuse and sin He can see. I imagine
the unbelievable pain He witnesses in the domestic fights, the tears
of women, the fear of children, the despair of men. I wonder about the
addicts and the homeless, wandering and desperate. He sees all of this
with perfect clarity. How His great heart must yearn to bring them love
and peace and redemption.

But the eyes of the Lord also see the lives and hearts of those who
trust in Him. He sees the homes where dads and moms are kneeling
to pray for their children and where little kids go to bed listening to
Bible stories, where His people prepare to rest in His care.

Tonight when you go to sleep, remember that the eyes of the Lord
are looking at everything in the world, and rejoice that you are in His
vision.

Lord, keep me in Your sight.
Thank You for choosing to watch over me. Amen.

Path Director

*Trust in the LORD with all thine heart; and lean not unto thine
own understanding. In all thy ways acknowledge him,
and he shall direct thy paths.*
PROVERBS 3:5–6 KJV

God does not have a director's chair, but He is the ultimate choice if you need direction.

If you've ever been part of a theatrical production, you know that the most important person, more so than the actors, is the director. His or her expertise and skill and instincts will either make the final presentation a success or a failure. An excellent director with a mediocre cast will put out a great show. A mediocre director with an excellent cast will deliver an average experience. The director breathes life into the parts and the acting by the way he or she explains the mood and inspires the actors and coaches the scenes. If the direction is great, those involved can perform well.

We often forget this in our spiritual lives. Even with a great script and wonderful directions (the Bible), we cannot produce a good outcome without the divine Director. If a part is missing, He knows what to do. If the setting changes, He can help us adjust. If the other actors abandon the show, He knows what to do. He is the key to our success.

Whatever you are facing on the stage of your life today, God can help you play it well. Turn to Him. He always has time for the cast, and you were chosen for this specific part.

*Lord, please direct my life and my actions
and words today. In Jesus' name, amen.*

Beautifier

*He hath made every thing beautiful in his time: also he hath
set the world in their heart, so that no man can find out the
work that God maketh from the beginning to the end.*
ECCLESIASTES 3:11 KJV

The beauty God is perfecting in us will be completed in His time, not ours. It is an eternal beauty, one that doesn't fade with age.

The apostle Peter gave this counsel to Christian women: "Let your adorning be the hidden person of the heart with the imperishable beauty of a gentle and quiet spirit, which in God's sight is very precious" (1 Peter 3:4 ESV).

God is working in us the kind of beauty that actually gets better with age. It doesn't fade but becomes more vibrant and more like the One who created us.

I used to wonder how I could be beautiful in Christ's image since I am a human woman and He came to Earth in the form of a human male. But then I realized that the beauty He is working in me transcends the skin and is formed in the heart, and He knows just how to shape that to the gender He gave me.

You and I were chosen for womanly beauty. Let's be patient while God finishes the work.

Lord, make me beautiful in Your way and in Your time. Amen.

Transformative Living

Do not be conformed to this world, but be transformed by the renewal of your mind, that by testing you may discern what is the will of God, what is good and acceptable and perfect.
ROMANS 12:2 ESV

I love home decorating stores and decorating magazines. And yes, I confess that I am susceptible to the newest decorating trend. When I first married, the country style was in, complete with geese—I went for that in my kitchen. Then I transitioned from that to apples, and friends and family bought me apple-themed items until I was tired of them. I tried the primitive approach for a while, using aged and distressed items with lots of muslin and candle lamps and such. Then I picked up some bits of shabby chic and modern farmhouse.

I find it kind of funny to look back at how I have been influenced by the changing currents of the culture. But it is more serious when culture affects other parts of our lives. The Bible instructs us to be settled and established in our faith so that we are not carried about with "every wind of doctrine" (Ephesians 4:14 ESV). We need not be continually reshaped by the popular ideas in culture about life and morality and eternity, but rather be transformed in an ongoing manner through our constant relationship with Jesus.

We were chosen to live called-out lives, not in the world's mold but in His.

Lord Jesus, You lived in the world but not as part of its harmful philosophies and ideas. Keep me as I try to follow Your example. Transform me by Your grace. Amen.

Fullness of Joy

You make known to me the path of life; in your presence there is
fullness of joy; at your right hand are pleasures forevermore.
Psalm 16:11 esv

On her wedding day, my daughter was radiant. It was the culmination of months of preparation and planning; the pinnacle of her three years of dating the man she loved and the day every girl looks forward to for her whole life long. She was beautiful. And the thing that made her so abounding with joy was the fact that he was there, and after that day, she would be in his presence (so to speak) forever.

We are the bride of Christ although the wedding has not yet occurred. But when it does, we will have overflowing joy in His presence. I have never yet seen a bride who dreaded her wedding day. There is something about being in the presence of the one you love that makes your heart sing.

God the Father is making preparations for the big day. Jesus, the Groom, has paid the bride price for our redemption and has left us His love letter, the Bible, to reassure us of His love. The Holy Spirit is the divine wedding agent, making sure all things are in readiness. When the time comes, Jesus will come to get us, and then we will know that fullness of joy. There is nothing better than being chosen to be His.

Lord Jesus, I am waiting for the day when I can be in Your
presence forever. Thank You for loving me. Amen.

Deliverance from Fear

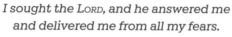

I sought the Lord, and he answered me
and delivered me from all my fears.
PSALM 34:4 ESV

I am scared of spiders.

The way they skitter across the floor and jump out from crevices and hide from the light gives me a creepy-crawly feeling. I know that God made them for a purpose, but it seems to me that they were probably less terrorizing before sin entered the world.

Perhaps you are frightened of bats or mice or ferrets. I don't like any of those either! And most of us are not too fond of snakes, even the harmless ones.

The psalmist David had been in a frightening situation of his own—an occupant in the house of King Abimelech, trying to avoid being killed. After he pretended to lose his mind, they let him go and he was saved from tragedy. He sang Psalm 34 to the Lord in thankfulness.

Most of us will never have an experience like that. At least, I hope not. But there will be times in our lives when we will have to combat fear. In those instances, God will be with us. He may not remove the fearful thing, but He will give grace and wisdom as we face it.

What fears do you face on a daily basis? Declining health? Loss of your marriage? Cancer? Losing your home? Your children's decisions? All these things can paralyze us and make us unable to carry on.

Turn to the One who can help you overcome your fear and meet the challenge.

Father in heaven, You delivered Your servant David,
and I know You can deliver me. Today I bring to You
this fear: [name fear]. Thank You for Your grace. Amen.

Endurance Just for You

No temptation has overtaken you that is not common to man.
God is faithful, and he will not let you be tempted beyond your
ability, but with the temptation he will also provide the
way of escape, that you may be able to endure it.
1 Corinthians 10:13 esv

At more than one point in my life, I joined Weight Watchers. I needed to lose weight and get healthy, and the temptations were so great that I thought group accountability would help.

Weight Watchers had a winning idea when they devised a plan to help their members endure temptation. It is silly to think that a normal person would never be tempted to overeat again or to choose an unhealthy option. So at the meetings I attended, we planned for holidays and big family dinners. We knew temptation would happen, and we needed a game plan to follow when it did. This boosted our chances for victory!

In the Christian life, we are aware that temptations will happen. We are not idealistic enough to believe that we will never be tempted. But with the help of the Holy Spirit, we can have a spiritual game plan and be ready to meet temptation. Second Corinthians 2:11 says that we are "not ignorant of [Satan's] devices" (kjv). We know the tricks he likes to use on us. But God is faithful, and He has chosen us for victory!

Lord, give me discernment today so that I may recognize
temptation and be prepared in the Spirit to be
victorious! In Jesus' name, amen.

Lights and Strongholds

The Lord is my light and my salvation; whom shall I fear?
The Lord is the stronghold of my life; of whom shall I be afraid?
PSALM 27:1 ESV

Lighthouses are spectacular structures. They vary in design and height, but wherever they are, towering above a lake or inlet or bay, they command respect and add beauty. Many lighthouses are made of stone or brick; they need to be sturdy in composition since they are often subjected to fierce storms because of their locations. Many times they are designed with an adjoining house where the lightkeeper lives. But the most important part of the lighthouse is the light. It is a life-saving device, meant to give mariners their bearing and help them avoid dangerous shoals. Some are still in use today, though not as many as in times past. Many are now national landmarks, valued for the good they have done and the history they reflect.

The psalmist looked to the Lord as to a lighthouse. As a sailor could be confident when he saw the powerful beam of the lighthouse, so could David be confident in the illumination God provided. We have no need for fear when we can see where we are going. Satan wants to get us confused in the dark, but God says for us to move closer to the light He shines.

What do you need light for today? Pick up His Word and ask Him for light.

You are my Light, O Lord. Shine on me today
and show me the path of safety. Amen.

He Who Answers

*"Call to me and I will answer you, and will tell you great
and hidden things that you have not known."*
JEREMIAH 33:3 ESV

I am a compulsive phone answerer. My husband is not. If my phone
rings, I usually answer it unless I am involved in something that makes
talking impossible. Maybe it comes from being a firstborn who plays
by the rules—if you can answer, answer. Maybe it's my innate curiosity.
In any case, I usually answer.

And you and I know the people in our lives who will answer if we
call them. Some will let it go to voice mail (and it's always full and
can't receive more messages). Some will answer if they recognize the
number. Some will call right back. Some won't even know you called
until you happen to talk to them the next time. We are all different
and approach our technology in different ways.

I'm glad that God is a committed answerer. He never stalls us or
takes a note to call us later. He tells us to call on Him and He will answer.

Your world may be in chaos today. Perhaps nothing is settled and
you are afraid. You haven't let anyone know what is going on with you.
Remind yourself that you are chosen to receive God's help and reach
out to Him. He has promised to be listening for you.

*Lord, I lift my voice to You today.
Show me the way to go. In Jesus' name, amen.*

Walking through Fire

"When you pass through the waters, I will be with you;
and through the rivers, they shall not overwhelm you;
when you walk through fire you shall not be burned,
and the flame shall not consume you. For I am the
LORD your God, the Holy One of Israel, your Savior."
ISAIAH 43:2–3 ESV

Fire has always been both useful and harmful. A blaze that warms campers can turn into an inferno that destroys homes. The match that lights a candle can ignite a curtain. How it is used determines the effect of fire.

In the Bible, fire is used as a symbol of God's power and direction, such as in the burning bush that Moses saw and the pillar of fire that guided the Israelites at night. But fire was also used to indicate trials and troubles, such as the fiery furnace into which the young Hebrew men were thrown in the book of Daniel.

Perhaps this verse from the book of Isaiah is referring to that. Do you remember the story? The king peered into the furnace and saw four men, not three. And when they were removed from the furnace, miraculously kept alive by God, there was not even the smell of smoke on them (Daniel 3).

As God's daughters, we are chosen to experience His presence and deliverance in the roughest times of our lives. If you are walking through a fire today, you can be assured that God is there with you.

Father, thank You for being with me in the flames today. Amen.

The Controlling Spirit

For God gave us a spirit not of fear but
of power and love and self-control.
2 TIMOTHY 1:7 ESV

Sometimes we talk about mind over matter. What we mean is that our minds are powerful and can control us. We have moments in life when we choose to do something regardless of how we feel about it. Yet fear is a powerful motivator. It can cause us to react in ways that are irrational or even dangerous. Having a solid and sensible emotional balance is important.

I wonder if Deborah in the Old Testament experienced fear when she agreed to march with Barak into battle against Israel's enemies (Judges 4). Perhaps she did. But she also knew that the God of Abraham, Isaac, and Jacob was on their side, and they could not be defeated if He was for them.

God does not give us fear. Fear comes from Satan. It arrived after Adam and Eve sinned. And now it winds its dark tentacles around us, trying to control us.

But the Spirit that comes from God, the Holy Spirit, is stronger. We must give Him control of our emotions and our thoughts. Then we can experience His power and love and self-control.

Lord, fill me with Your Holy Spirit today,
and help me not to walk in fear. Amen.

Looking for the Joy

Weeping may tarry for the night,
but joy comes with the morning.
PSALM 30:5 ESV

Things seem worse at night. Trials seem harder, arguments are more heated, sickness is worse, hope seems gone. But in the morning, though nothing may have changed, the sun's brightness gives us renewed confidence and hope that things can be better.

In the Bible, night or darkness is often used to symbolize sin or the condition of people who are living in sin. When Judas left the Last Supper to betray Jesus, it was night (John 13:30). Paul tells the Roman Christians that drunkenness often takes place at night (1 Thessalonians 5:7). On the other hand, Christians are admonished to be children of the day (1 Thessalonians 5:5; Romans 13:13).

Night is also used to signal a time when we feel desolate and alone. But God is the same at night as He is in the day. David said in Psalm 139:12 that the darkness and the light are both alike to God. Job said that God gives "songs in the night" (Job 35:10 ESV).

God created the night for the benefit of humankind. He created our bodies to respond to the lack of light so that we could rest. He put a rhythm into our world of night following day. When we are in fellowship with Him, we don't have to fear the night. He is Lord of it too.

Heavenly Creator of all, thank You for nighttime.
Help me to remember that You made it for my good.
I lay all my problems in Your hands. Amen.

Sufficient Grace

[The Lord] said to me, "My grace is sufficient for you, for my
power is made perfect in weakness." Therefore I will boast
all the more gladly of my weaknesses, so that
the power of Christ may rest upon me.
2 CORINTHIANS 12:9 ESV

An old saying goes, "Enough is as good as a feast." It means that if everyone has enough, that's as satisfying as having a bountiful table that no one is eating.

When it comes to the grace of God, we know that there is always enough. In fact, there is more than enough.

More than one type of grace is mentioned in the Bible. *Prevenient grace*, or grace that goes before, makes us aware of our sinful condition, drawing us toward Christ. *Saving grace* or redeeming grace works in our hearts at the moment of salvation, enabling a new birth in Christ and making us part of God's family. *Keeping grace* strengthens us as we endure temptations. And *enabling grace* gives us divine empowerment in our trials and suffering.

The apostle Paul had some type of weakness or infirmity. Bible scholars have discussed and debated it for years. No one really knows what it was, but it was trying to him. Nevertheless, Paul said that God had enabled him through divine grace to boast in his suffering because Christ's power was evident through it. What a lesson for us as we encounter our own types of weaknesses.

Father, my life is the one You have given me, and You
know the infirmities I have. Let Your grace rest on me,
and glorify Yourself in my weakness. Amen.

The Sentinel

Don't worry over anything whatever; tell God every detail of your needs in earnest and thankful prayer, and the peace of God which transcends human understanding, will keep constant guard over your hearts and minds as they rest in Christ Jesus.

PHILIPPIANS 4:6–7 PHILLIPS

If there is any admonition in the Bible that many of us are guilty of violating on a regular basis, it's this one. Not that we intend to disobey God's Word, but we so often get caught up in the trap of worry. And there is such a fine line between concern and anxiety and stress that, at times, it's hard to distinguish one from the other.

I know that God understands that not worrying is a challenging action for us to take. That's why He addresses it often. Remember that Jesus told His listeners not to worry about having clothing or food or drink (Matthew 6:31). God knows that in our temporal world, with so much to take up space in our minds, we are prone to carry these concerns with us and not trust Him. And many times our worries include things far beyond the basics of food and shelter. But regardless of the type of need, we are told not to worry, not to let our recognition of need turn to anxiety.

The promise Paul was inspired to give us is that the peace of God will guard our hearts and minds through Christ Jesus. The Greek word used here for "guard" implies a type of military guard, a sentinel protecting a garrison from invasion. This is the type of strong protection that our Lord gives us when we trust Him.

Lord Jesus, You told us to trust the Father in heaven for all our needs. Please guard my heart and mind with Your truth. Amen.

The Process

*When all kinds of trials and temptations crowd into your lives my
brothers, don't resent them as intruders, but welcome them
as friends! Realise that they come to test your faith
and to produce in you the quality of endurance.*

JAMES 1:2–3 PHILLIPS

Most of the events in our lives happen in a process. A few joys are immediate and spontaneous, but many of our earthly blessings take time. Babies develop in the womb in a process, children grow to maturity in a process, marriages grow strong bonds in a process, gardens produce vegetables and plants produce blooms in a process.

When it comes to our spiritual lives, we must realize that they are in process also. We should not expect our spiritual maturity to be a microwave moment or an overnight miracle. God uses the trials and experiences of life to grow us in the faith.

So when we realize that we are in the midst of being tested, we should rejoice, says the apostle James. It is then that we realize that we are in the growth process.

Most of the time the growth process isn't appealing because God uses unattractive things to make us better. But if we stay faithful, these things will produce in us a quality of endurance that will help us to make it through to the end and see Him someday.

*O God, I am in the middle of a trial. Remind me that it is
a process You are using to grow my faith. In Jesus' name, amen.*

The Wings that Protect

He shall cover you with His feathers,
and under His wings you shall take refuge.
PSALM 91:4 NKJV

The words of Psalm 91 have been a comfort for countless generations of people. Its promises of protection and comfort and presence are God-breathed and pull us closer to the One who is always faithful in our difficulties.

Verse 4 especially has wonderful significance. The first phrase reminds us of Jesus' words about Jerusalem when He wept because He wanted to protect and nurture her as a mother hen gathers her chicks under her wings (Matthew 23:37).

The second phrase uses a word for wings that can mean bird wings but can also refer to the flap or border of a robe. It was the word used when Ruth asked Boaz to spread his "wings" over her (the flap of his robe; Ruth 3:9). It is also the word used in Malachi 4:2 (KJV) speaking of the coming Messiah who will arise "with healing in his wings."

Our God wants us to understand that He is our protector and keeper. He gathers us to Himself and preserves us in the time of trouble.

Maybe today you are facing an extreme situation and you feel all alone. Take courage and lean into the promise of this verse. If you have trusted Christ, you are a chosen daughter and He will protect you.

Holy Lord, I run to Your protection today.
Cover me with Your protecting and healing wings. Amen.

The Peace Giver

*"The mountains shall depart and the hills be removed, but My
kindness shall not depart from you, nor shall My covenant of peace
be removed," says the LORD, who has mercy on you.*
ISAIAH 54:10 NKJV

God promised the land of Canaan to Abraham and his descendants
through Isaac, the child of promise. But the people disobeyed and were
taken captive and spent generations in foreign lands. Sporadically, they
would return and live in peace and the worship of Jehovah for a while
and then the cycle would repeat. Finally, after the fall of Jerusalem in
AD 70, the twelve tribes of Israel were scattered over the entire world
and the Holy Land was destroyed and inhabited by others. After the
devastating losses in the Jewish population during the Holocaust,
God's people all over the world began to return to their native land.
There were great challenges and many conflicts, but they kept coming from north and south and east and west. In 1948 Israel became an
independent nation. And they will never give it up.

Someday Jesus will stand on the Mount of Olives and enter through
the Eastern Gate of Jerusalem, fulfilling prophecy. God is not done with
the holy events destined to take place in Palestine.

God has made a covenant of peace with all of us because of His
Son, Jesus. The payment for our sins has been made, and we can be
reconciled to Him if we only believe.

*Lord Jehovah, You are great and Your words come to pass.
Thank You for Your covenant of peace. Amen.*

The Proclaimer

"The Spirit of the Lord GOD is upon Me, because the
LORD has anointed Me to preach good tidings to the
poor; he has sent Me to heal the brokenhearted,
to proclaim liberty to the captives, and the
opening of the prison to those who are bound."

ISAIAH 61:1 NKJV

On a sleepy day in the synagogue in the village of Nazareth, the usual worship rituals were taking place. Then the time came for one of the men to read from the Torah. Something was different as a young man covered His head and reached for the scroll from Isaiah and began to read, "The Spirit of the Lord is upon Me. . ." (Luke 4:18 NKJV).

Yes, that man was Jesus, and this really happened. Luke wrote about it in his Gospel (Luke 4:16–22). He said that all the eyes in the room were fixed on Jesus as He finished reading, sat down, and announced, "Today this Scripture is fulfilled in your hearing" (NKJV). All the people marveled.

Can you imagine the electrifying atmosphere in the synagogue that day? When Jesus comes, everything is different.

Our world today needs this message more than ever. We need the power of Jesus to give good news and to heal the brokenhearted and to set addicts free and to open the prisons that many are in—prisons of depression and sexual immorality and substance abuse. We need hope in our world, and Jesus brings it.

Maybe you are the one who needs to hear these words today. If you are struggling with something that no one else knows about, don't give up! Turn your eyes and look at the One who proclaims His mighty mission to save, heal, and deliver. His power is at work today. Reach out for His mercy and grace.

God, I am needy today. Bind up my wounds, heal me,
and set me free. In Jesus' name, amen.

The Wisdom Distributor

If any of you lacks wisdom, let him ask of God, who gives to all liberally and without reproach, and it will be given to him.

JAMES 1:5 NKJV

None of us will ever have the opportunity that King Solomon had. God came to him in a dream and said that he could request whatever he wanted. Solomon asked for wisdom, and God granted it (1 Kings 3:5–10). Solomon is still known as the wisest man who ever lived.

We do, however, have unlimited access to the God of the universe who has promised to give us wisdom whenever we ask.

Every day we face situations for which we need the wisdom of the Father—relationships with friends, parenting, communication with our husbands, and conversations with service attendants and sales associates. We may be the only voice of kindness and wisdom that someone hears in a day. What an opportunity!

Using wisdom in speech doesn't necessarily mean bland words either. At times, the Lord may want us to use wise, stirring speech. Paul told the Colossians that their speech should always be full of grace but also "seasoned with salt" (Colossians 4:6 NKJV). It might have a little sting to it, but it will preserve the hearer. Obviously, we need the Holy Spirit's guidance, but there is a place for mentioning the name of Lord in a public setting or saying something overtly Christian. Let's be open to His leading.

Dear Lord, please give me wisdom today and use my speech for Your purposes. In Jesus' name, amen.

The Victory of Resisting

*Therefore submit to God. Resist the devil
and he will flee from you.*
JAMES 4:7 NKJV

In the European theater during World War II, there was a strong resistance movement. This sometimes loosely gathered and sometimes tightly organized movement aided the cause of the Allies from inside the occupied countries. They were people from every walk of life who wanted freedom to be preserved and were against the principles of fascism. They were used as couriers, saboteurs, guides, informants, and spies. They felt a duty to resist evil.

This is a historical example of what it means to resist in a good way. Many times we think of resisting with a negative connotation because it seems to imply rebellion and selfishness. But resistance to evil is always a good thing, and it demands resolve and stamina.

For the resistance movement, it was a long war. Many of the operatives died while working against the Nazi regime. But their comrades didn't give up.

And we can't give up in our resistance to Satan. He will try again and again. He won't give up the war just because we resist one time. He will attack again in another place; he will try new tactics. He will set traps for us.

But the Word of God promises that the devil will flee if we are strong in Christ and continue to resist his suggestions. He cannot make us sin, because Jesus is greater and truth always wins over lies.

*Lord, make me strong so that I can resist the tactics
of the devil. I submit myself to You. In Jesus' name, amen.*

Faithful to Forgive

*If we confess our sins, He is faithful and just to forgive us
our sins and to cleanse us from all unrighteousness.*
1 JOHN 1:9 NKJV

When a child is caught disobeying, it is vital to help him or her understand that the way to avoid punishment is not to repeat the offense. It might take a little while for those who are more strong-willed, but the important thing is for the parent to be more determined than the child. If a parent lets the child win, then what she has communicated is that Mom will wear down after a while and she really doesn't mean what she says. The child will take that lesson with him or her into adult life and figure that God can be manipulated as well.

So the point for children and for all of us is to understand that we should not disobey or sin. But the Bible tells us that if we do, our Father is faithful to forgive. As a mother, I was faithful to forgive too. I would never hold my child's action against him or her in the future. But that did not cancel the consequences. And neither does it with God.

Forgiveness restores fellowship with God, but we may still suffer the earthly consequences of our rebellion. So, with this in mind, let's engage today with a determination to obey the Holy Spirit's voice.

*O Lord, thank You for forgiving me when I ask,
but help me to obey when You speak to me. Amen.*

The Freedom Giver

"Therefore if the Son makes you free, you shall be free indeed."
JOHN 8:36 NKJV

When I was a child, my family used to listen to the radio program *Unshackled*. It was produced by a rescue mission in the city of Chicago and featured the true stories of people whose lives had been transformed by the Gospel. Some of them were associated with the mission; others were from far away, but they had been set free from their painful memories and binding addictions.

Addictions are Satan's way of using our longings for love against us. All of us have an area of vulnerability, a weakness for something that can become a pathway to addiction. But underneath the actual thing to which one is addicted is an emotional need. Satan then deceives us into thinking that indulging this desire will fill the hole in the heart. But it doesn't, and we feel worse than before. So, the next time, we must have more of it to try to compensate for the emptiness and then more and more until the thing has us in a vise-like grip.

The Bible says that the Son of God can set us free. He holds the keys to any chain and to any prison door. You were chosen by Him to be free, and He will rescue you if you will turn to Him instead of to Satan's lies. Feeding the addiction doesn't make you whole, but He will.

*Lord Jesus, please show me any area of my life where I am
turning to something besides You. Set me free
by the power of Your shed blood. Amen.*

The Supplier

*My God shall supply all your need according
to His riches in glory by Christ Jesus.*
PHILIPPIANS 4:19 NKJV

You may have heard it said that America runs on trucks. If you drive much on the freeways and interstates of our nation, you can vouch for that. Semitrucks with trailers dominate the roadways, carrying products for all manner of retailers. Without the trucking chain, our economy would be shuttered. Truckers are the suppliers of our day.

A century ago, trains primarily formed the supply chains. Crisscrossing the country on shiny rails, these smoking steel monsters transported products and people all over the nation.

God doesn't need a truck or a train, but He knows how to get supplies to His people when they need them. We've all heard stories of miracles. Maybe you've experienced one of those. Our family had a supply miracle in the form of a church board member who showed up at our parsonage door with bags of groceries one afternoon. We were in a particularly difficult financial situation at the time, and the bills were more than our resources that week. But God showed up.

This verse was originally written to a generous church who had given to a specific need, and the apostle Paul was reassuring them that God would take care of them. He will do the same for us in His own way and time.

*Father, thank You for running the supply chain of heaven.
I trust Your provision for me. Amen.*

The Benefits Package

*Bless the L*ORD*, O my soul; and all that is within me, bless His holy name! Bless the L*ORD*, O my soul, and forget not all His benefits: who forgives all your iniquities, who heals all your diseases, who redeems your life from destruction, who crowns you with lovingkindness and tender mercies, who satisfies your mouth with good things, so that your youth is renewed like the eagle's.*

PSALM 103:1-5 NKJV

When interviewing for a new job or different position, it is important to inquire about the benefits package. Comprised of the details about compensation, holidays, vacation days, sick time, and insurance resources, this information may help one decide whether to take the job. Some jobs don't offer a great hourly wage or salary, but the benefits make up for it.

For those who serve the Lord, there is no way to lose. First of all, He offers salvation from sin and an eternal home in heaven. But then He piles on the side benefits. David lists them: forgiveness, healing, redemption, kindness, mercy, extra good things.

And of course, many other advantages to living a clean, righteous life.

We are not like the fickle crowds who followed Jesus just for the loaves and fish (John 6:26), but it is good to recognize all the blessings of serving the Lord and to thank Him for them. We have been chosen to receive the fulfillment of many promises.

*Heavenly Father, You give me benefits every day,
and I am thankful. Amen.*

The One Who Is for Us

In face of all this, what is there left to say? If God is for us,
who can be against us? He that did not hesitate to spare his
own Son but gave him up for us all—can we not trust such a
God to give us, with him, everything else that we can need?
ROMANS 8:31–32 PHILLIPS

Most of us can count on at least one person always being "for" us. For many of us, our moms have been "in our corner" since day one. They always believe in us, hang our kindergarten art on the fridge, tell us we'll be the best one on the team someday, go to all our piano recitals, give us cookies when we make bad grades, and declare that we are the smartest in the school. Then when we are adults and on our own, they call us to make sure we're doing okay, give us laundry and cooking advice, and brag that their grandkids are the most beautiful of all. Moms are the world's best human allies.

But the best ally of all, of course, is God. The apostle Paul asked rhetorical questions in Romans 8 to help us understand just how much God wants us to succeed. Surely, if the Father would go to all the personal anguish and sacrifice to give His Son up for crucifixion, He is fully invested in our total redemption. He won't withhold from us anything that we need to live a victorious life in Christ.

Father God, thank You for Jesus.
I trust You for everything else I need. Amen.

Inseparable Love

*I have become absolutely convinced that neither death nor life,
neither messenger of Heaven nor monarch of earth, neither what
happens today nor what may happen tomorrow, neither a power
from on high nor a power from below, nor anything else
in God's whole world has any power to separate us
from the love of God in Jesus Christ our Lord!*
ROMANS 8:38–39 PHILLIPS

All of us want love that lasts, love that goes the distance, love that will come to us regardless of obstacles. We want the love that will scale Mount Everest and swim the English Channel and hike the Grand Canyon to get to us. Every once in a while, we think we glimpse a glimmer of something like that. It usually happens in the gaze of the groom at a wedding or in the eyes of a new mom or on the face of a grandparent—suddenly we see a little spark that reminds us that strong, true love exists.

The apostle Paul was certain that such love existed in the heart of our heavenly Father. Under the inspiration of the Holy Spirit, he penned these magnificent words in Romans 8, telling us that nothing in heaven or on earth can separate us from the incredible love God has for us. If our sin couldn't do it and all the demons of hell couldn't shake it and all the diabolical plans of Satan can't sway it, then surely nothing living or dead, royal or common, natural or supernatural can do it either.

*Father in heaven, I celebrate this promise
of Your unshakable love for me. Amen.*

Justice for the Poor and Needy

*I know and rest in confidence upon it that the Lord will
maintain the cause of the afflicted, and will secure justice
for the poor and needy [of His believing children].*

PSALM 140:12 AMPC

If you're like me, you are sometimes troubled by the thought of believers in other lands who are suffering. Some don't have enough food to feed their families. Some have lost their homes. Some are imprisoned for their faith. Some have been disowned by their families because of Christ. Some are lying in filth and squalor after being tortured for their Christian testimony.

It seems unfair that many of us have comfort and ease in comparison to their lack. We know that God holds the answers to all these hard questions. Verses like this one are reassuring because they say that God has not forgotten His children who suffer. Someday all will be right, and believers will be rewarded in great measure for their endurance for His name's sake. We cannot know the mind of God nor the reasons He chooses one life for one and another for another. But it is our responsibility to accept what has been given and use it to the full for His kingdom.

*Strengthen Your children in other lands, O Lord.
I know You are faithful and just to all. Amen.*

Slow to Anger

The Lord is gracious and full of compassion, slow to anger and abounding in mercy and loving-kindness. The Lord is good to all, and His tender mercies are over all His works [the entirety of things created].

PSALM 145:8–9 AMPC

A tradition says that people with red hair have fiery tempers. While I have reddish highlights in my hair, I have never been accused of being a redhead. But I have had my moments of fiery temper.

Some people are said to have a "hair trigger," meaning they are very easily irritated. Others are said to carry a "chip on the shoulder," meaning they tend to be easily offended. Some people we "tiptoe" around so that we don't set off "fireworks." And so we have ways to identify characteristics in people that describe their propensity to anger.

The psalmist says that the God of heaven is "slow to anger." Imagine that. The one Being in the whole universe who has the absolute divine right to be angry with all of us is slow to anger. Those who believe that God is a cosmic bully have it all wrong. And that is Satan's fault, for they have believed his lies. But we who know the truth take comfort in this promise, and we know that the Lord's tender mercies are over all who trust in Him.

Lord God, I am awed at the love You show. Help me to be like You in being slow to anger with others. Amen.

Everlasting Kingdom

Your kingdom is an everlasting kingdom, and Your
dominion endures throughout all generations.
PSALM 145:13 AMPC

No earthly kingdom is unending.

The Egyptian pharaohs wanted immortality, and they created gargantuan statues and pyramids and monuments to their own glory and then had themselves mummified so they could reign in the next world.

The emperors of China built the Great Wall and planned for their dynasties to go on forever.

The Romans designed glorious temples and coliseums and statues to tell the story of their greatness to the world.

The Nazis thought they were ushering in the Third Reich, the third thousand-year reign, and set about erecting great buildings and parade grounds in which to hold ceremonies and rituals to their own honor.

None of these regimes have remained. They have all been conquered by others.

But the reign of Jesus, the King of kings and Lord of lords, will never end. When He comes again to Earth to set up His throne, He will rule in righteousness and justice. We have been chosen to be part of that reign. And He keeps His promises.

O Lord, let Your kingdom come and Your will be done. Amen.

He Is Near

The Lord is near to all who call upon Him,
to all who call upon Him sincerely and in truth.
PSALM 145:18 AMPC

When my husband served as a hospice chaplain, I remember him talking about the gift of presence. Often when people are grieving, they don't need an explanation or a long, flowery speech. Instead, they can benefit from merely the presence of someone who cares. That is not to say that there isn't a time and place for words and food and prayers. But in the darkest moments, sometimes the presence of a friend is what matters. Not being alone. Sitting in silence together.

The Bible tells us that the Lord is near to those who call on Him. Often we have needs that make us feel separated from others. Sometimes these needs are too difficult to explain in words to another human being. But the Lord who made us understands us. He draws near to us when we call.

When my children were little and scared of the dark, just my presence in the room was enough to help them go to sleep. Sometimes I would sit in their rooms or lie down on their little beds until they became drowsy. I think the Lord sometimes does that for us. When we call out, "Father, I'm scared," He comes and sits on our bed until we drift off to sleep. His presence is enough to calm us.

Dear Father, thank You for Your presence in my
lonely and fearful moments. Amen.

Holy Advocate

*The L*ORD *opens the eyes of the blind; the L*ORD *raises those who are
bowed down; the L*ORD *loves the righteous. The L*ORD *watches
over the strangers; he relieves the fatherless and widow;
but the way of the wicked He turns upside down.*

PSALM 146:8–9 NKJV

If you've read Dickens's classic *A Christmas Carol*, then you know that
the main character, Ebenezer Scrooge, is a self-centered miser who
leaves everyone else to their own devices and expects the same for
himself. He cares for no other man, woman, or child. He believes every
person is responsible for their own welfare, and is not inclined to give
of his hard-earned wealth to contribute to another's comfort, even if
they have been disadvantaged and are in need.

In creating this abominable character, Charles Dickens manages
to juxtapose him against all that is beautiful and wonderful at Christmas and expose the extreme heartlessness of such a person. So, when
Scrooge has a miraculous change of heart, we rejoice with him because
we know how bad he has been.

God is, of course, the holy opposite of the evil Dickens tried to
portray. He cares for all, and those who are needy are especially close
to His great heart. The psalmist lists some of them in these verses—the
blind, the "bowed down," the strangers, the fatherless, the widows. God
is their advocate and their defender. And those who tend to them on
earth are doing His work.

*Lord, thank You for caring for those who are needy.
Show me how I can be an advocate for them. Amen.*

The Sustainer

*Sing to the L*ORD *with thanksgiving; sing praises on the harp to our God, who covers the heavens with clouds, who prepares rain for the earth, who makes grass to grow on the mountains. He gives to the beast its food, and to the young ravens that cry.*
PSALM 147:7–9 NKJV

In the place where I live, "green spaces" are valued. Because it is a fast-growing area with housing developments springing up everywhere and businesses moving into the surrounding lots in large numbers, the residents are concerned that some patches of grass and trees and field are left untouched.

While it is important to care for the resources God has given us and to be kind to the animals He created, it is also vital to keep things in proper perspective. We may value what is created, but we should value the Creator more.

The Bible tells us that it is the Lord who changes the atmosphere and sends rain and makes the grass to grow. He feeds the animals and birds. What we do may affect the earth, but we cannot destroy the ozone layer or bring about climate change or make a species of animals extinct without His permission. Christian stewardship requires that we are wise in our decisions that affect the earth, but it also dictates that we acknowledge the Sustainer of all things as Lord.

Father God, You tend the earth
and sustain it. I'm thankful. Amen.

The Snow Giver

He gives snow like wool; He scatters the frost like ashes;
He casts out His hail like morsels; who can stand before
His cold? He sends out His word and melts them;
He causes His wind to blow, and the waters flow.
PSALM 147:16–18 NKJV

Many people dislike snow. The next time a snowstorm is predicted, just listen to the groans and complaints. Now, I understand that snow can cause travel difficulties as well as hazards and hardships for those who work outdoors. It is understandable that no one wants to be inconvenienced. But even those who can stay indoors seem opposed to snow.

The Bible tells us that God gives the snow. He scatters the frost and casts out the hail. He is in charge of the seasons, and He chooses to let us experience both heat and cold. We need the change for reasons only He truly knows. Perhaps our psyches just need the variety. And of course, the seasons help the ground to rest and then replenish for the growing cycle.

You may never turn into a lover of winter, but you can still appreciate the God who controls the weather. The next time a snowstorm is predicted where you live, give a little bit of thought to the One who is sprinkling it down upon the earth, and remember that you are in His care.

Lord of heaven, I delight in the world You made.
Thank You for the seasons. Amen.

Chosen by Name
Her Name Was Abishag

*So they sought for a lovely young woman throughout all
the territory of Israel, and found Abishag the Shunammite,
and brought her to the king. The young woman was very
lovely; and she cared for the king, and served
him; but the king did not know her.*

1 KINGS 1:3–4 NKJV

Young Abishag had one of the oddest occupations named in the Bible. She was carefully selected from all the other young women to serve King David in a unique way. In his old age, the king could not keep warm, even though his attendants piled blankets on him. So they came up with the idea that body heat would be the best thing to try. I'm not sure why none of the women in the royal harem were fit for the job, but it was decided that the job should go to a beautiful virgin. The king would not have intimacy with her, but she would be considered to be married to him so that no impropriety could be accused.

I have wondered about Abishag. Her name means "my father wanders." Maybe she was the daughter of a traveling man. I have questioned how she felt about this arrangement. What young woman in her right mind would want to be married to an ancient king and only as a warming agent? Did she have other dreams for her life? Was there a young man whom she hoped to marry?

Maybe your life has thrown you a curveball and you feel a little like Abishag—this is not what you bargained for. Today, remember that nothing that happens to us is unseen by the One who can redeem anything we bring to Him, even living in the harem of King David.

*Lord, give me grace to live this life and peace in the
things I cannot control. In Jesus' name, amen.*

Her Name Was Hephzibah

Manasseh was twelve years old when he became king,
and he reigned fifty-five years in Jerusalem.
His mother's name was Hephzibah.

2 KINGS 21:1 NKJV

You shall no longer be termed Forsaken, nor shall your
land any more be termed Desolate; but you shall be
called Hephzibah, and your land Beulah; for the LORD
delights in you, and your land shall be married.

ISAIAH 62:4 NKJV

Queen Hephzibah was the wife of King Hezekiah and the mother of Manasseh. Her name means "my delight is in her" and is used to refer to the Promised Land and also in reference to the Church, the bride of Christ.

To be delighted in is a great joy. For a woman, there is hardly a greater pleasure than to see the delight in the eyes of the man she loves. Admittedly, this is, to a great degree, a choice on his part. But nevertheless, she can invite his delight in her in various ways.

In the symbolism of Christ and Church in marriage, the apostle Paul describes the respect a woman should have for her husband (Ephesians 5:22–23). This attitude in her will invoke a response in him.

And even those women who are not in an earthly marriage can be the recipients of this kind of love as the bride of Christ. One day the whole world will know that He is delighted with us.

Lord, thank You for choosing me as part of Your bride,
the Church. I want You to delight in me. Amen.

Her Name Was Joanna

Now it came to pass, afterward, that He went through every city and village, preaching and bringing the glad tidings of the kingdom of God. And the twelve were with Him, and certain women who had been healed of evil spirits and infirmities—Mary called Magdalene, out of whom had come seven demons, and Joanna the wife of Chuza, Herod's steward, and Susanna, and many others who provided for Him from their substance.
LUKE 8:1–3 NKJV

Joanna was a woman whose husband had a royal position. She had been healed by Jesus of some sort of affliction, though it is not known whether it was a demonic possession or a physical illness. She was among the women who supported Christ's earthly ministry and was one of the women who prepared spices to anoint His body after the crucifixion. Her name means "Jehovah hath shown favor."

Depression and mental illness are common challenges, yet they are shrouded in shame and secrecy because there seems to be a stigma attached to them. It is comforting to realize that women who knew Jesus when He walked on earth faced some of the same kinds of difficulties that we do today. Perhaps Jesus healed Joanna of an emotional imbalance, or perhaps it was some other kind of ailment. We do know that the woman who touched the hem of Jesus' robe was suffering from a menstrual condition (Matthew 9:20). Jesus, the Great Physician, has time and compassion for us all and understands our most delicate and sensitive problems.

Lord Jesus, help me always to remember that nothing I suffer is too insignificant to bring to You. Amen.

Her Name Was Martha

*Martha welcomed Him into her house. And she had a sister
called Mary, who also sat at Jesus' feet and heard His word.
But Martha was distracted with much serving, and she approached
Him and said, "Lord, do You not care that my sister has left me
to serve alone? Therefore tell her to help me." And Jesus
answered and said to her, "Martha, Martha, you are
worried and troubled about many things."*
LUKE 10:38–41 NKJV

The name Martha means "lord" or "master," and since she was the firstborn in her family, the name fits. Martha was very capable and organized with a gift for hospitality. Her home would have been the one that was tastefully decorated and Jesus apparently loved to stay there. Her siblings, Lazarus and Mary, were also friends of Jesus, and it's probable that they shared many fun evenings together.

Martha was probably an extrovert compared to her sister, who seems to be the introvert. The Bible implies that both of them were accustomed to sitting at the feet of Jesus and learning (it says Mary "also" sat). But perhaps Martha, with her ever-efficient, practical side, was thinking about the meal she needed to serve and so left to tend to her cooking. Jesus' reply to her complaint about the unfairness of the situation should not be taken as unkind. He loved this family and would not embarrass Martha who had done so much to serve Him. One commentator said His words could be interpreted this way: "Martha, you are busy with many courses when one dish would be quite sufficient. Mary has chosen the best dish, which shall not be taken away from her."

That sure puts a different perspective on the story of Mary and Martha. Which one of these women are you most like? You can't change that, and God doesn't want you to. We need Marthas! But make sure you are intentionally choosing what is better when you have the opportunity.

*Lord Jesus, give me the wisdom not to be so distracted with
practical things that I neglect to spend time with You. Amen.*

Her Name Was Rizpah

*Now Rizpah the daughter of Aiah took sackcloth and spread it
for herself on the rock, from the beginning of harvest until
the late rains poured on them from heaven. And she did
not allow the birds of the air to rest on them by
day nor the beasts of the field by night.*

2 SAMUEL 21:10 NKJV

Rizpah's story is one of the most tragic in the Bible. She was one of King Saul's concubines. Her name means "a hot stone" or "a baking stone."

She is most known for her vigil over the slain bodies of the king's sons after they were executed in vengeance for Saul's treatment of the Gibeonites. The corpses were hung on trees and left there to rot and be devoured by birds.

Rizpah determined that this would not happen. She set up camp on a nearby rock and became the guardian of the slain sons. From the beginning of harvest until the late rains, she defended them from the vultures and the jackals; she witnessed their decay in the elements. Finally, when the rains came, she went home, and King David had the bones gathered up and buried with Saul and Jonathan in the family tomb.

This woman showed unbelievable stamina in a horrible situation. But when a mother is grieving, she will do anything to protect what remains of her precious child.

Today you may be called to do something unpleasant as a service to your King. Remember Rizpah, and stand at your post.

*Father in heaven, thank You for loyal love and the
determination to do what is right. Amen.*

Her Name Was Salome

*Then the mother of Zebedee's sons came to [Jesus] with her sons,
kneeling down and asking something from Him. And He said
to her, "What do you wish?" She said to Him, "Grant that these
two sons of mine may sit, one on Your right hand and the
other on the left, in Your kingdom." But Jesus answered
and said, "You do not know what you ask."*
MATTHEW 20:20–22 NKJV

Salome has the dubious honor of trying to get favored positions for her sons.

We don't know what went on before this, but we do know that at one time, James and John were referred to as the "Sons of Thunder" (Mark 3:17 NKJV). Evidently they had a taste for action and retribution. Perhaps this spoke to a family proclivity for outspokenness and a passion for advancement. Whatever the reason, Salome comes with her boys and asks for special favors.

We don't know if Jesus was personally irritated with her or not. But He did tell her that she wasn't aware of the significance of what she was asking. The positions of right and left of the throne would be given to those who suffered and served much. This mother was unknowingly asking for her sons to suffer.

Sometimes we are irritated with others' requests for God's help in their children's lives. But let's remember that not every mom understands the gravity of her words, and let's be careful of our own petitions to Him.

*Father God, grant me the discernment to pray in
Your will and not offer foolish petitions. Amen.*

Chosen for Wisdom

Don't Be This Woman

To deliver you from the immoral woman, from the seductress who flatters with her words, who forsakes the companion of her youth, and forgets the covenant of her God. For her house leads down to death, and her paths to the dead; none who go to her return, nor do they regain the paths of life.

PROVERBS 2:16–19 NKJV

The woman in these verses from Proverbs is not named as an actual person; rather, she is a composite of evil traits, a portrait of what every woman should avoid.

The wise writer of Proverbs was warning his son against the advances of a seductive woman who flatters with her words and does not honor God. While it is a wonderful thing for a woman to care for her God-given beauty and to dress attractively and becomingly, it is a sin against her Maker and against others for her to use her body and her beauty in ways that focus the attention on her sensual attributes. That kind of intimacy is reserved for her husband alone and not to be shared on the streets. A woman can be pretty without being provocative. Our culture has lost this understanding. The word "hot" is used today as a compliment, though in actuality it is a euphemism for "sexy" and has a connotation of a dog in heat.

These verses tell us that a seductive woman leads a man to death. This strong admonition is wisdom for us. We are chosen to honor our beauty as an act of worship to our Creator.

Father, help me today to use my beauty in ways that honor You and not me. Amen.

Consider the Ant!

Go to the ant, you sluggard! Consider her ways and be wise,
which, having no captain, overseer or ruler, provides her supplies
in the summer, and gathers her food in the harvest. How long
will you slumber, O sluggard? When will you rise from your sleep?
A little sleep, a little slumber, a little folding of the hands
to sleep—so shall your poverty come on you like a
prowler, and your need like an armed man.
PROVERBS 6:6–11 NKJV

For one of my children's birthdays, we bought an ant farm. It was all cleverly contained in a plastic structure that allowed us to see what was happening. We had to order the ants and have them shipped to us. We were supposed to be able to see them making their tunnels and building their colonies. The whole thing started off well, but the ants must not have liked our home, or we didn't do something right. Before too long, they stopped moving and died. And that was the end of our ant-gazing.

But for those who have seen ants scurrying around a mound of dirt outside, you know that they will carry more than their weight in crumbs and never seem to take a break. Yet scripture implies that the ants observe the seasons, so perhaps they lie around more in the winter.

The lesson for us is to be diligent in completing the work God has chosen for us.

Lord, help me to be as committed to my work as the ant is to
hers. My choices today will make the difference. Amen.

God Hates This Stuff

*These six things the L*ORD* hates, yes, seven are an abomination to Him: a proud look, a lying tongue, hands that shed innocent blood, a heart that devises wicked plans, feet that are swift in running to evil, a false witness who speaks lies, and one who sows discord among brethren.*
PROVERBS 6:16–19 NKJV

It's not uncommon to hear someone use the phrase "I hate that." What normally follows is something the person strongly dislikes, but rarely is it something that is actually hated. We use the expression to voice our trivial irritations in everyday life.

But God uses this expression to mean exactly what it says. He hates or abhors the things in this list. And no wonder! These things are the core of wickedness—pride, lies, murder, plotting evil, mischief makers, liars, gossipers, and troublemakers. These things are not only an affront to God but are an offense against one's fellow man.

The writer of Proverbs wants us to understand that God has strong feelings about the laws He has given us. They are not suggestions or recommendations. He expects our obedience to His commands. And when we honor Him by being obedient, life for us and our neighbors is so much better.

O God, I want to avoid doing anything on this list!
Put a Holy Spirit alarm in me today. In Jesus' name, amen.

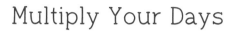

Multiply Your Days

*"The fear of the L*ORD *is the beginning of wisdom, and the knowledge of the Holy One is understanding. For by me your days will be multiplied, and years of life will be added to you. If you are wise, you are wise for yourself, and if you scoff, you will bear it alone."*

PROVERBS 9:10–12 NKJV

Reading the stories of centenarians and the changes they have observed during their lifetimes is fascinating. Quite often they are asked to share the secret of their long lives. These vary greatly, but most of them are simple answers about not holding grudges or eating fruit every day or drinking water. Truth be told, they probably don't know the reason they have lived that long. It wasn't something they planned. It was simply the number of days God had planned for them.

The Bible tells us that having reverence for the Lord is a good way to start a long life. Of course, many godly people have died young. We won't understand all the reasons for that until eternity. But we know that ordering our lives by God's principles positions us to experience health and protection.

Not one of us knows the actual number of days God has allotted to each of us (Psalm 139:16). He has planned them, and He watches over them. But in the time we have today, we must choose to honor the work He has begun in us by gaining knowledge of the Holy One. That is always a health-giving commitment!

Lord, help me to use my day to increase my knowledge of You and to bless someone else. Amen.

Honor and Discretion

A gracious woman retains honor, but ruthless men retain riches. . . . As a ring of gold in a swine's snout, so is a lovely woman who lacks discretion.
PROVERBS 11:16, 22 NKJV

Being discreet is not thought of as a beauty secret in much of our culture. The popular notion of femininity today is drawing attention to the body and having a flashy attitude. Perhaps the advent of selfies has contributed to the development of the latter—today's teen girls are apt to pucker their lips and make V signs across their eyes in an attempt to appear sassy. But the fashion world has pooh-poohed discretion for over a century.

Beginning with the flappers of the Roaring Twenties who flaunted their ankles (of all things!), the world of style began to erase former restrictions and flirt with seduction. Up until that time, there had always been "loose" women and tavern girls, but the typical woman would not have considered trying to attract male eyes to her body in skimpy clothing. The rebellion against gender roles and restrictions began a movement that continues to this day, and at times the boundaries seem almost entirely gone.

The fact remains that God, the Creator of womanly beauty, says to us that a lovely woman without discretion is as incongruous as a pig wearing a gold ring—out of place, ridiculous, and apt to get smeared in the mud.

Creator God, develop in me the grace of discretion, and help me honor You with my femininity. Amen.

Be a Soul Winner

The fruit of the righteous is a tree of life,
and he who wins souls is wise.
PROVERBS 11:30 NKJV

If you've played the game of LIFE, you know that your profession is chosen for you depending on where you land on the game board. This scenario might be truer to life than one might think since many of us end up doing something other than what the earning of our degree prepared us for, and it sometimes happens in the most random ways! However, the profession you are given then dictates the salary you will earn for the remainder of the game. Some make more than others, and that will, in turn, either help you or hinder you as you circle the board, paying bills, suffering financial reverses, and marrying off your "children."

One profession I've not seen on the game board is that of "soul winner." And true, it's usually not a paid profession, but it is a job that all believers should attempt to make their own.

The old-time preachers used to talk about soul winning, but it isn't mentioned much today. But there are other kinds of outreach that we do focus on when we come to church. In fact, many of the programs that churches undertake for their communities should have, as their ultimate goal, the introduction of people to Jesus. For that to be effective, we need to approach our children's ministries and Bible studies and small groups with prayer. We need the power of the Holy Spirit at work. This is the only way that lives will be touched and changed.

O God, give me a passion for those who are unbelievers.
Help me to win souls to You. Amen.

Don't Be Stupid

Whoever loves instruction loves knowledge,
but he who hates correction is stupid.
PROVERBS 12:1 NKJV

God's Word is blunt. It zeroes in on where we need to improve. Look at the punch of this verse if you don't believe it.

I love books. And since books are in libraries, I love libraries. I can get overwhelmed surveying all the shelves with volume after volume and thinking about how many of them I'd like to read.

My father took me to get my first library card when I was a child. This library was an ornate structure, a Carnegie Library, stately and proud. The smell of old books captivated me, and I've never gotten over it. Maybe that makes me a lover of knowledge on one level.

But God says that if I really love knowledge, I will love instruction. Whew! That's another story. It's difficult to receive reprimands and rebukes and instruction. It's more fun to do things my way. But I need the humility of listening to someone else explain something; I need the discipline of doing something another way.

In your life today, there will probably be an occasion for you to listen to instruction. Remember, as you grit your teeth and do it, that you are proving that you're not stupid! And God is pleased with your effort.

Lord, I don't like instruction, so help me to learn
humility and submission by listening. Amen.

Don't Cause a Stink

An excellent wife is the crown of her husband,
but she who causes shame is like rottenness in his bones.
PROVERBS 12:4 NKJV

Even if you're not married, you have seen enough married people to realize the undeniable truth of Proverbs 12:4. Some men seem to be able to handle life well; they are well thought of, pleasant, and capable. Others seem grumpy and sad and never available.

As much as we'd like to blame it all on the men, the truth is that many times the attitude of the husband can be partially caused by his wife.

Of course, no one can pin all the guilt on a husband or wife, but it is undeniable that one's spouse has a huge bearing on the attitude one has. And this seems especially true of husbands.

In the beginning, God said that it wasn't good for man to be alone (Genesis 2:18). Since that time, the old adage is true—"A wife can either make or break her husband." While he is responsible for his own actions, the power of a woman is so great that she can actually improve the man he is by her love for him.

And, on the other hand, she can be like an infection that starts decay in his soul and works its way out until everyone can tell something is wrong.

If you have a husband, think today about how you can make him shine—not stink.

O God, give me a heart that wants to help my
husband shine brighter than ever. Amen.

Discipline Your Child

He who spares his rod hates his son,
but he who loves him disciplines him promptly.
PROVERBS 13:24 NKJV

When Dr. James Dobson wrote a book titled *Dare to Discipline*, it took the parenting world by storm. After a few years of the passive approach of Dr. Spock, American parents wanted a real answer for the defiance they were facing in their children.

God knows the human heart, so He instructs parents to use firm discipline with their children. In fact, He says that if you don't, then you don't truly love your child. Love involves doing what is best for the other person even if it hurts. The proof of love is not that you withhold discipline but that you do it for a greater purpose.

The Bible gives an example of a father who did not discipline his sons. Eli the priest had two sons who were an abomination to the Lord. They even committed sexual sin with women who came for religious rituals. God told Eli that they would die because he had not restrained them (1 Samuel 3:13). It is probable that Eli's passivity started in their childhood, because right parenting and discipline when children are young decreases the likelihood of their rebellion as young adults. It may not eliminate it, but it should at least temper it.

If you have children, determine to discipline them well and promptly as the scripture says. Everyone, including them, will be glad someday that you did.

O Lord, give me wisdom to be a godly parent today
and to discipline my children well. Amen.

Give It to Them Softly

*A soft answer turns away wrath, but a harsh word stirs up
anger. The tongue of the wise uses knowledge rightly,
but the mouth of fools pours forth foolishness.*
PROVERBS 15:1–2 NKJV

The Word of God runs crossgrain to cultural wisdom. Since the Bible is God's unchanging truth and the world has come so far from truth, the gap is wide. Many today have no idea of the life-changing principles that are foundational for relationships.

More and more, the approach of people in conflict is to match the level of vitriol they are hearing from the other side. As both parties do this, tension escalates, and often irreparable damage is done.

God advises another way. He tells us to answer harshness with softness. This is not to say that we should be soupy sweet in such a way as to be deliberately irritating. Rather, we are to answer without that "bite" in our words, even though we are being attacked. This kind of approach will help to turn off the anger download and maybe salvage the relationship.

How much kinder and clearer our world would be if we took this advice!

*Lord Jesus, You are my example, for You never used words
wrongly. Help me follow Your example. Amen.*

Enjoy Your Snack

*Better is a little with the fear of the L*ORD*, than great treasure*
with trouble. Better is a dinner of herbs where
love is, than a fatted calf with hatred.
PROVERBS 15:16–17 NKJV

A Thanksgiving feast is a wonderful thing! How beautiful is a table spread with a turkey and all the fixings and lots of pies and cakes for dessert. Then the family gathers around and gives thanks to God and the dishes begin to rattle as the crowd digs into the food.

But a huge family dinner can be a terrible affair if there is strife and tension and division around the table. In such a case, God says it's better to have frozen pizza on a paper plate!

What makes a feast is not really the food, but the faces around the table. Anything can be enjoyed when there is harmony and joy. With her intuition for family feelings and her keen awareness of body language and verbal communication, the mom of the family may sense if something is amiss before the others do. Often what is needed is someone to steer the conversation away from volatile topics and toward less sensitive ones. While this is not always possible, it's worth a try.

As the mother in the family or the woman at the table, you have a unique skill set that God has given you to bless the ones around you. Do your best!

Lord, give me the insight to know how to bring
harmony to our family feasts! Amen.

Chosen for Miracles

A Miracle for Today

But when Jesus heard [that the synagogue ruler's daughter was dead], He answered him, saying, "Do not be afraid; only believe, and she will be made well." When He came into the house, He permitted no one to go in except Peter, James, and John, and the father and mother of the girl. Now all wept and mourned for her; but He said, "Do not weep; she is not dead, but sleeping." And they ridiculed Him, knowing that she was dead. But He put them all outside, took her by the hand and called, saying, "Little girl, arise." Then her spirit returned, and she arose immediately. And He commanded that she be given something to eat. And her parents were astonished, but He charged them to tell no one what had happened.

LUKE 8:50–56 NKJV

We don't know her name, but this twelve-year-old girl in Luke's account had her life totally changed by the power of Jesus. I wonder what became of her. What about her adult life? Did she become a Christ follower? What did she think when she heard that the man who had raised her up was now being executed? Could she have been part of the early Church?

Maybe you, like her, had an encounter with Christ as a child. Today you're an adult and the glow of that experience has faded. You've faced other things that have rocked your faith. You need to find out who Jesus is for yourself again.

The Christ who raises bodies also raises souls. Bring your adult wondering to Him today.

Lord, I need help for my doubts and fears.
Please do a miracle of grace in me today. Amen.

181

Packing a Lunch

One of his disciples, Andrew, Simon Peter's brother,
said to him, "There is a boy here who has five barley
loaves and two fish, but what are they for so many?"
JOHN 6:8–9 ESV

We've all heard the story of Jesus using a little boy's lunch to feed over five thousand people. But I wonder about the mom who packed it for him.

Did she get up that morning and send with him all they had? He was excited, after all, because he was going to see the great teacher Jesus. He needed something to eat because the day would be long. She sent him all she could. He was a growing boy. He could certainly eat all of it.

Maybe she went with him to hear the Master. If she did, she witnessed the miracle herself. But maybe she only heard about it later. Maybe her friends came to tell her. "Do you know what happened today?" Maybe her son, excited and weary, told her all about it when he returned.

I used to dread packing lunches when my kids were in school. It was one of those daily chores that hasn't much glamour but a lot of tedium. But I never packed a lunch that Jesus blessed like that one!

Today, whether you're packing your own lunch or one for someone else or maybe packing a suitcase or a computer bag, offer whatever it is to the Master and let Him use it in a unique way.

Father in heaven, please multiply my little today
and make it much as I share it with others. Amen.

Opening the Gate

*And when he knocked at the door of the gateway, a servant girl
named Rhoda came to answer. Recognizing Peter's voice, in her joy
she did not open the gate but ran in and reported that Peter was
standing at the gate. They said to her, "You are out of your mind."
But she kept insisting that it was so, and they kept saying,
"It is his angel!" But Peter continued knocking, and when
they opened, they saw him and were amazed.*
ACTS 12:13–16 ESV

Rhoda was a servant. A big prayer meeting was going on for the apostle
Peter. James had already been beheaded, and the Christian community
feared that Peter would be next. While they were praying, an angel
released Peter from prison and guided him to the home of Mary, John
Mark's mother. And when Peter knocked, Rhoda answered.

Perhaps, being a servant, Rhoda first had to report to her mistress
about who was at the door. But the people in the meeting didn't believe
her. Finally, they checked out what she was saying and discovered it
was true.

There are many gates in our lives—places where God puts us in the
path of a miracle. We can open the gate and experience His power, or
we can let the gate stay shut. Don't assume life is going to be the same
old thing today. Go, answer the gate. Things may be about to change.

*Lord, You know the needs in my life. Give me the determination
to open the gate to a new opportunity. Amen.*

Gathering the Pots

"Go outside, borrow vessels from all your neighbors, empty vessels and not too few. Then go in and shut the door behind yourself and your sons and pour into all these vessels. And when one is full, set it aside." So she went from him and shut the door behind herself and her sons. And as she poured they brought the vessels to her. When the vessels were full, she said to her son, "Bring me another vessel." And he said to her, "There is not another." Then the oil stopped flowing. She came and told the man of God, and he said, "Go, sell the oil and pay your debts, and you and your sons can live on the rest."

2 Kings 4:3–7 esv

The husband of the woman in our passage was dead, and the creditors were coming for her sons. She needed a miracle. She consulted the prophet and did what he said. As a result, she had enough money to pay off her debt and save her sons.

Life is hard for single moms. At times, they may feel like the creditors are coming to take away their children. You might be the answer to some mom's prayer. God could use you to work her miracle. Offer to babysit. Give her a gift card. Be there for a chat. Watch God work through you.

Heavenly Father, open my eyes to ways
I can be a blessing to a single mom today. Amen.

Raising Up Tabitha

Now there was in Joppa a disciple named Tabitha, which, translated, means Dorcas. She was full of good works and acts of charity. In those days she became ill and died, and when they had washed her, they laid her in an upper room. Since Lydda was near Joppa, the disciples, hearing that Peter was there, sent two men to him, urging him, "Please come to us without delay." So Peter rose and went with them. And when he arrived, they took him to the upper room. All the widows stood beside him weeping and showing tunics and other garments that Dorcas made while she was with them. But Peter put them all outside, and knelt down and prayed; and turning to the body he said, "Tabitha, arise." And she opened her eyes, and when she saw Peter she sat up. And he gave her his hand and raised her up. Then, calling the saints and widows, he presented her alive. And it became known throughout all Joppa, and many believed in the Lord.

Acts 9:36–42 esv

The Bible doesn't tell us what Tabitha's illness was, but it seems to have been fairly aggressive. Nevertheless, someone believed she could be healed. They didn't bury her right away but sent for the apostle Peter. He prayed and told her to get up, and she did.

Imagine her surprise! Here she was finally getting to rest and Peter prayed her back to life so she could go to work again! Her miracle was for others because they needed her. Yours may also be for someone else.

Dear Lord, keep me going as long as I need to in order to accomplish the purpose for which You chose me. Amen.

Exalting Jesus as Lord

*As we were going to the place of prayer, we were met by a slave girl
who had a spirit of divination and brought her owners much gain
by fortune-telling. She followed Paul and us, crying out, "These men
are servants of the Most High God, who proclaim to you the way
of salvation." And this she kept doing for many days. Paul, having
become greatly annoyed, turned and said to the spirit, "I command
you in the name of Jesus Christ to come out of her."
And it came out that very hour.*

ACTS 16:16–18 ESV

The slave girl in our passage was a pawn of Satan and a money-making tool for her masters. Scripture doesn't tell us her name, but it does say that she was afflicted by an evil spirit. When the men of God came to town, she was drawn to them, but her cries were loud and irritating and disruptive. Finally, Paul turned to her and commanded the unclean spirit to come out. And, by the power of Jesus, it did.

It seems as though this slave girl was a young teen. Maybe she didn't remember any other life. But like the man in the tombs whom Jesus healed, we can imagine that she was soon in her right mind. Her healing caused Paul and Silas to be thrown into prison, but from that predicament a new church of believers was born.

Any good that is done in my life or yours must bring God glory. Our miracles of grace make us trophies in His honor. We were chosen to exalt Him, now and forever.

*Father in heaven, glorify Yourself in my life,
both now and in the life to come. Amen.*

Scripture Index

More Inspiration for Your Beautiful Soul

God Calls You Forgiven

In a culture that fills your head and heart with lies about your value in the world. . .there is One who calls you forgiven.

And He can be trusted. His Word is truth.

This delightful devotional—created just for you—will encourage and inspire your soul with deeply rooted truths from God's Word. Each devotional reading and heartfelt prayer will assure you that you are truly forgiven—because God says so. . .and His Word is unchanging! Each of the 180 readings in *God Calls You Forgiven* will help you to grow in your faith and increase your self-confidence as you become the beautifully courageous woman the heavenly Creator intended you to be!

Flexible Casebound / 978-1-64352-637-9 / $12.99